The Battle of Hurricane Bridge

March 28, 1863

With the Firmness of Veterans

PHILIP HATFIELD, PHD

35th Star Publishing
Charleston, West Virginia
www.35thstar.com

Copyright © 2019 by Philip Hatfield, PhD.
All Rights Reserved.
Printed in the United States of America.

No part of this publication may be reproduced, distributed or transmitted in any form or by any means, including photocopying, recording, or other electronic or mechanical methods, without the prior written permission of the publisher, except in the case of brief quotations embodied in critical reviews and certain other noncommercial uses permitted by copyright law.

ISBN-13: 978-0-9965764-7-5
ISBN-10: 0-9965764-7-9

35th Star Publishing
Charleston, West Virginia
www.35thstar.com

On the cover: Captain James W. Johnson, Co. A, 13th West Virginia Volunteer Infantry. West Virginia State Archives; Regimental flag of the 13th West Virginia Volunteer Infantry. West Virginia State Museum; Brigadier General Albert G. Jenkins. Library of Congress; Regimental flag of the 8th Virginia Cavalry. National Civil War Museum, Richmond, Virginia.

Cover design and interior layout by: Studio 6 Sense – www.studio6sense.com

The Battle of Hurricane Bridge

March 28, 1863

With the Firmness of Veterans

PHILIP HATFIELD, PHD

Dedication

*The Battle of Hurricane Bridge is dedicated
to the loving memory of my parents,
who instilled in me a lifelong love of history.*

Calvin Lee Hatfield

Freda Jane Hatfield

"...the enemy appeared in force and opened a furious fire upon us simultaneously on three sides from as many different hills, owing to the high elevation of which, and unfinished condition of our works, exposed our men to a most galling cross fire, which they withstood and returned with the firmness of veterans."

Captain James W. Johnson
13th West Virginia Volunteer Infantry

Union Commander
at Hurricane Bridge
March 28, 1863

Contents

Introduction XIX
1 – The Kanawha Valley During the Civil War 1
2 – Outpost at Hurricane Bridge 29
3 – The Earthen Fort at Hurricane Bridge 51
4 – Field Hospital at Hurricane Bridge 63
5 – Confederates in the Hills 73
6 – Battle at Hurricane Bridge, March 28, 1863 99
7 – Jenkins Attacks at Point Pleasant, March 30, 1863 133
8 – After the Battle at Hurricane Bridge 157
Epilogue: The Second Battle at Hurricane Bridge 167
Appendix A: Order of Battle 175
Appendix B: 13th West Virginia Volunteer Infantry
    Company A Muster Roll 177
Appendix C: 13th West Virginia Volunteer Infantry
    Company B Muster Roll 183
Appendix D: 13th West Virginia Volunteer Infantry
    Company D Muster Roll 189
Appendix E: 13th West Virginia Volunteer Infantry
    Company H Muster Roll 193
Appendix F: 8th Virginia Cavalry, Company C
    Troops present March 28, 1863 199
Appendix G: Union Casualties at Hurricane Bridge 207
Name Index 209
About the Author 213

Illustrations

County Map of Virginia and West Virginia, 1863 .... XXIII-XXIV
1829 Map Showing Extension of Kanawha Turnpike XXV
Captain Hurston Spurlock, Co. H, 16th Virginia Cavalry 5
2nd Lieutenant Oliver W. Griswold, Co. H, 13th WV Infantry 6
Jacob Dolson Cox 14
Confederate Guerillas, *Harper's Weekly*, July 20, 1861 15
Governor Francis H. Pierpont 18
Lieutenant-Colonel James R. Hall, 13th WV Infantry 23
Captain John V. Young, Co. G, 13th WV Infantry 24
Colonel William R. Brown, 13th WV Infantry 33
Captain James W. Johnson, Co. A, 13th WV Infantry 34
Captain Milton Stewart, Co. B, 13th WV Infantry 35
1st Lieutenant Lovell C. Rayburn, Co. B, 13th WV Infantry 35
2nd Lieutenant Samuel S. Mathers, Co. A, 13th WV Infantry 36
2nd Lieutenant George Snowden, Co. D, 13th WV Infantry 37
Unidentified Officer, 13th WV Infantry 37
Sergeant Robert H. Davis, Co. A, 13th WV Infantry 38
Hurricane Bridge State Historical Marker. 42
Hurricane Bridge and State Historical Marker 43
Private Samuel Gaskins, Co. E, 13th WV Infantry 45
Sketch of typical earthen fort in the Civil War 55
Reproduction of Civil War era earthen fort 56

Modern Hurricane Bridge area	57
View of western heights, Union fort area	58
View of western heights, houses removed	59
1829 Map Showing Extension of Kanawha Turnpike	60
1829 Map Showing Extension of Kanawha Turnpike, Enlarged	61
Dr. Samuel G. Shaw, 13th WV Infantry Surgeon	69
Albert Gallatin Jenkins	83
Colonel Milton J. Ferguson, 8th Virginia Cavalry	84
Colonel James Corns, 16th Virginia Cavalry	85
Lucien C. "Cooney" Ricketts, Co. E, 16th Virginia Cavalry	90
Captain Jonathan Hankins, Co. C, 16th Virginia Cavalry	90
Sergeant Daniel C. Lovett, Co. G, 8th Virginia Cavalry	91
1st Sergeant Calvin Cyfers, Co. E, 16th Virginia Cavalry	92
Private John A. Miller, Co. G, 8th Virginia Cavalry	93
Private Mark Hale Sesler, Co. C, 8th Virginia Cavalry	94
Private Charles Perrow, Co. C, 8th Virginia Cavalry	95
13th West Virginia Infantry 1862 regimental colors	104
Letter by Corporal John H. Hess, Co. D, 13th WV Infantry	106
Map of Hurricane Bridge Battlefield	110
Variations of Whitworth Rifle with Globe site, Telescopic Site	111
Whitworth .451 caliber bullet (11.5 mm diameter)	112
Side View of the Whitworth .451 Bullet	112
1842 U.S. Springfield Rifled Musket, .69 caliber, socket bayonet	114
1861 Richmond Musket, Rifled, .69 caliber	114
1862 Austrian Lorenz Rifle	114
John S. Cunningham	118

Grave marker of Private Henry Sands 119

Minie' Balls recovered at Hurricane Bridge (.58, .69 caliber) 126

Minie' Ball recovered at Hurricane Bridge (.58 caliber) 126

Horseshoe recovered at Hurricane Bridge 127

Union knapsack rivet recovered at Hurricane Bridge 127

Camp lead recovered at Hurricane Bridge 128

Axe head recovered at Hurricane Bridge 128

Various bullets recovered at Hurricane Bridge 129

Brigadier General Albert G. Jenkins 140

Captain John D. Carter, Co E., 13th WV Infantry 141

2nd Lieutenant Charles T. Latham, Co. E, 13th WV Infantry 142

Colonel Rutherford B. Hayes, 23rd Ohio Infantry 143

2nd Lieutenant John H. Rosler, Co. E, 13th WV Infantry 144

1st Lieutenant William N. Hawkins, Co. E, 13th WV Infantry 145

Mason County Court House 152

Regimental Flag of the 13th West Virginia Vol. Infantry 165

Preface

As a very young child, I played in the fields around the small town of Hurricane, West Virginia not knowing that a once bitter and violent struggle took place there during the Civil War. My passion for history, in particular the American Civil War, began when my parents took me to visit the Gettysburg National Battlefield Park. Listening to the historians describe the events which transpired there, and reasons for them, captivated me. The result eventually morphed into an indelible, tireless pursuit of understanding the causes, struggles, and implications of that war, particularly in my home state of West Virginia.

As an adult, my fascination with the March 28, 1863, fight occurring at Hurricane Bridge only intensified. Collecting every fact, anecdote, folktale or bit of oral history I could find, a new understanding formed of not only the military operations during the battle, but also the people involved. Simply put, the further I dug into this story, the more obvious it became that what took place at Hurricane Bridge on March 28, 1863, was much deeper than previously thought. It has been said that when one is busy making history, there is little time to write it. As a result, historic research often initially relies on some level of speculation and oral tradition. However, as new evidence becomes available, the picture becomes much clearer and our understanding deepens.

Yet, the reader should also realize that even with new and factual information, we have only scratched the surface of what transpired at Hurricane Bridge. The same is also true for events occurring in the area of western Virginia that became West Virginia during the war period; much research is yet needed on the thirty-fifth state. It is my hope that by including as many original sources and other factual evidence to tell the story, readers will come to understand not only the unique perspectives of the soldiers who fought here, but also the experiences of the civilians involved who paid a dear price. Another, and no less critical goal, is to inform the reader of the larger military and political context in which the battle of Hurricane Bridge occurred, and the unique implications for this otherwise quiet, sleepy village.

For years, the March 28, 1863, fight at Hurricane Bridge was known as but a small skirmish, considered otherwise insignificant to the larger strategic picture of the Civil War, if not overlooked altogether. There are several original sources cited in this book written by soldiers present at Hurricane Bridge. They refer to it as both a "battle" and one citizen of Putnam County later called it an "engagement." What's the difference, one might ask? It has to do with not simply the number of soldiers involved, but also the ferocity, intensity and impact of what has taken place. Therefore, the conflict is referred to as a battle, not a skirmish, in this present work. Hopefully, in this context the reader will also recognize that what happened at Hurricane Bridge was much larger, yet more personal and malevolent than traditionally thought.

Indeed, it was a small affair in contrast to the massive battles fought in the larger theatres of the war. However, according to the men who fought there, it was indeed a "battle" and their lives and fortunes were at stake. Further, in this region the results enabled Union forces to maintain control of a crucial roadway, the James River and Kanawha Turnpike, which directly contributed to the Union holding a large portion of the area that became West Virginia. Ultimately, it is my hope that this small contribution will help preserve my hometown's rich history, and honor those who fought for principle.

Philip Hatfield, Ph.D.
Hurricane, West Virginia
April 9, 2019

Acknowledgments

I owe a great deal of thanks and gratitude to Scott Edwards, Mayor of the City of Hurricane, and the City Council of West Virginia for their support and belief in the importance of historic preservation. Mrs. Sandra Duke and Mr. Greg Williamson also; each kindly allowed access to private land for the author to conduct research. I also must thank Joe Geiger and his excellent staff at the West Virginia State Archives, notably Debra Basham and Aaron Parsons, who were extremely helpful. In addition, Catherine Rakowski and Jessica Eichlin at the West Virginia University Regional Library History Collection deserve many thanks. Cassandra Farrell, Senior Map Archivist Library of Virginia, and Chad Underwood, Special Collections Archivist Library of Virginia, are also owed a debt of gratitude for assistance locating maps and manuscripts for this project. Ron Allen and Betsy Allen at the Hurricane Breeze Newspaper also contributed the letters of Dr. Samuel G. Shaw. Amanda Larch edited the text and is due my gratitude, often making time for this project when she had many competing academic tasks.

Further, Sarah Pendleton at Carlisle Army History Education Center for assistance locating photographs, and Drew Gruber at the Civil War Trails group was also very helpful and instrumental in making the preservation effort at Hurricane Bridge a reality. Historian and Author Terry Lowry, a longtime friend and influence also deserves recognition for assistance locating areas on the battlefield of Hurricane Bridge of the Union camp and hospital sites. I owe much to Steve Cunningham of 35th Star Publishing also for support on this project (he worked many weekends with me at Hurricane Bridge in cold weather and mud digging for history) and a friendship spanning twenty-seven years. Steve ever reminds me that West Virginia Civil War history is largely a story untold and deserves serious study.

I must also thank my longtime friend, Irving Scarberry of Hurricane, for constructive feedback, with whom I spent many hours discussing history, re-enacting the Civil War, and walking the battlefield area at Hurricane Bridge, looking for clues to the past. No publication I produce is ever complete without thanking and remembering my wonderful parents, Calvin and Freda Hatfield, who are gone now, but will always live in my heart. They are the reason I developed a passion for Civil War History.

The following persons are also gratefully acknowledged for their contributions to this work: Neil Richardson, St. Albans Historical Society; Brett Kirby, Hurricane, West Virginia, who was willing to share artifacts recovered from Hurricane Bridge; Nathan Lucas, a life-long friend who provided information on the oral tradition related to Hurricane Bridge; in addition, these folks all provided key information: Kathy Haskins, descendent of Samuel Gaskins, 13th West Virginia Infantry; Keith Sesler, descendent of Mark Hale Sesler, 8th Virginia Cavalry; Debbie Cesta, descendent of John V. Young; Penny Hunt, descendent of William Wolfe, 13th West Virginia; Nathan Easter, descendent of Daniel C. Lovett, 8th Virginia Cavalry; and Sandy Miller Larch, descendent of John Miller, 8th Virginia Cavalry. Last but not least, thanks to my old friends, Scott Forloine and Mark Huffman, for contributing information related to Hurricane Bridge.

Introduction

On March 28, 1863, the otherwise quiet village of Hurricane Bridge in western Virginia found itself host to a five-hour long battle during the Civil War. The units engaged were four companies of the 13th West Virginia Volunteer Infantry, commanded by Captain James William Johnson, and Confederates of the 8th and 16th Virginia Cavalry, commanded by Brigadier General Albert Gallatin Jenkins, a former United States Congressman. Often referred to as the Skirmish at Hurricane Bridge, this small action is commonly thought to have meant little in the larger picture of the war.

However, there were significant military and political results from the affair than previously recognized. In the eyes of not only the soldiers who fought there, but also the civilians caught between the opposing forces, this small but furious battle had far reaching consequences. At a minimum, it forever connected the small village of Hurricane Bridge with the Civil War.

On April 17, 1861, the Virginia Assembly voted in favor of secession and joined the Confederacy. Earlier, pro-Union delegates from the forty-eight western counties had walked out of the Secession Convention and were planning to form a new state government favoring the Union; quite literally, the tentative state of West Virginia was formed from secession within secession. President Abraham Lincoln soon gave consent for the fledgling state to begin recruiting its own regiments for service in the Federal army in June 1861. These troops, while still technically Virginians, began to refer to themselves as West Virginians shortly after leaving Virginia. They are referred to as West Virginia troops herein to reduce confusion.[1]

THE BATTLE OF HURRICANE BRIDGE, MARCH 28, 1863

Why was it named "Hurricane Bridge?"

Located in Putnam County, in western Virginia, (now West Virginia), not far from the Kanawha River, lay the mouth of Hurricane Creek, so named by a group of early surveyors working for George Washington, who came to the area in 1774. They discovered the effects of a recent thunderstorm had laid several large trees in a long, symmetrical pattern at the creek's mouth, resembling that found along the path of a large hurricane, and hence named it Hurricane Creek. The small, quiet village located further south near Cabell County became known later as the Hurricane Settlement. The first European migrants settled there around 1778.[2]

This area was a busy trading and hunting post for Native Americans in the pre-colonial era, and eventually grew into something of a hub located in the area where Hurricane Creek crosses the James River Turnpike. (This is the area where modern U.S. Route 60 intersects with Midland Trail, i.e. State Route 34.) Hurricane Bridge appears on Virginia maps as early as 1811. It became known as Hurricane Bridge due to the large wooden and uncovered bridge spanning Hurricane Creek. That bridge was located in the same spot as the modern bridge, and not where the modern bridge crosses U.S. Route 60, as some writers have erroneously asserted. The community was later known as Hurricane Station upon completion of the single railroad track in 1873 and was re-named as the town of Hurricane by an act of the Putnam County Court after the results of a general election on October 30, 1888.[3]

The 1860 United States Census indicates there were ninety-nine homesteads reported in the Village of Hurricane Bridge and eight unoccupied buildings. Other sources indicated there were twelve farm houses and a few barns located near the immediate battle field area in March 1863; the others were located further northwest near modern Main Street in Hurricane, West Virginia.

Remains of two such structures were found in the northern corners of the same field where the modern era Hurricane Bridge Park is located, according to a 2017 archeological study. Subterranean remains of various wooden structures with stone foundations were discovered in that area, thought to be farm houses from the mid to late nineteenth century.

There were also remains of burned out stone fireplaces discovered in the area, consistent with Civil War era eyewitness accounts describing the burnt homes located near Hurricane Bridge. Archeological evidence recovered there also indicated the area was used as a pre-historic hunting ground and lithic tool production site by Native Americans during the Archaic Period. The area was not deemed eligible for the National Register of Historic Places, however, as it was not determined a part of the Civil War battlefield, which is located a few hundred yards south, and did not yield any significant artifacts which could contribute to scientific understanding of historic or pre-historic eras.[4]

One of the buildings located near Hurricane Bridge was a large, log frame building used as a school house, a meeting house and also as a church by both the Baptists and the Methodists. The church building was located about one mile south of where the modern railroad passes through South Main Street in Hurricane. Church records show that on May 26, 1860, the Baptists organized their church in that building with twenty-four members mostly from the Mt. Vernon, Mt. Salem, and Union areas. Two of those pioneer Baptist Church members were John and Rachel Griffith, the grandparents of Sergeant Lewis Griffith, who served in Company G, 13th West Virginia Volunteer Infantry.

That outfit was later assigned to the 11th West Virginia Volunteer Infantry, but in March 1863, Griffith was stationed at nearby Coalsmouth. (Modern St. Albans, West Virginia) Because the Baptist pastor was a circuit rider serving several congregations in the area, services were often held on Saturday afternoon or Sunday mornings. Many homes and other buildings at Hurricane Bridge were burned by the Confederates during the March 28, 1863, battle. The twenty-four Baptist church members did not attempt to re-organize until 1871; then they met in an old log building located on the southeastern corner of the present day First Baptist Church site on Main Street in Hurricane.[5]

One of the first people to settle in the Hurricane Bridge area was Jacob Reed Young. Born on August 26, 1790, he and his first wife, Nancy Stephenson, had seven children. Their home was located on the James River and Kanawha Turnpike near Sam's Fork and Snag Creek. His land was deeded to him by Lewis Tackett, one of the first settlers in the Kanawha Valley in the 1700s. One of those children was Captain John Valley Young, who commanded Company G, 13th West Virginia Infantry. He was born in 1813. Jacob and Nancy's youngest son, Samuel Early Young, was born in 1826, and later served in Company G with his brother during the 1864 Shenandoah Valley Campaign and at Petersburg in 1865. Another of Jacob's children, Alexander Young, was born in 1815. He married Sarah Ann Stephenson, Nancy's sister, and their home was located on the north side of the James River Turnpike just west of Coal Mountain. Captain Young's home was also in that vicinity. Nancy Young died when Jacob was aged twenty-seven years, and he re-married in 1869 (at age seventy years) to Cynthia Higginbotham.[6]

Known primarily as a stage-coach stop on the James River Turnpike, there were approximately five hundred residents in 1863. In addition to the twelve farm houses located in the battlefield vicinity, there was a general store, a flour mill, and also a larger house used as both a family home and tavern, located about three hundred yards from where the turnpike intersected with Midland Trail. It was a large home located on the ridge just south of the bridge spanning Hurricane Creek. It was accessed by a small road running east from the bridge along the ridge.

An 1815 map of Virginia shows a stage coach station on the Kanawha and James River Turnpike about three miles southeast of the present railway in modern Hurricane. Descendants of the family who owned the tavern have reported observing multiple bullet holes in the walls of the old house following the March 28, 1863, battle. They also recovered large quantities of bullets in the walls, and several clothing items from the 19th Century were found hidden within several walls inside the house. The building was destroyed in the early 1900's.[7]

INTRODUCTION

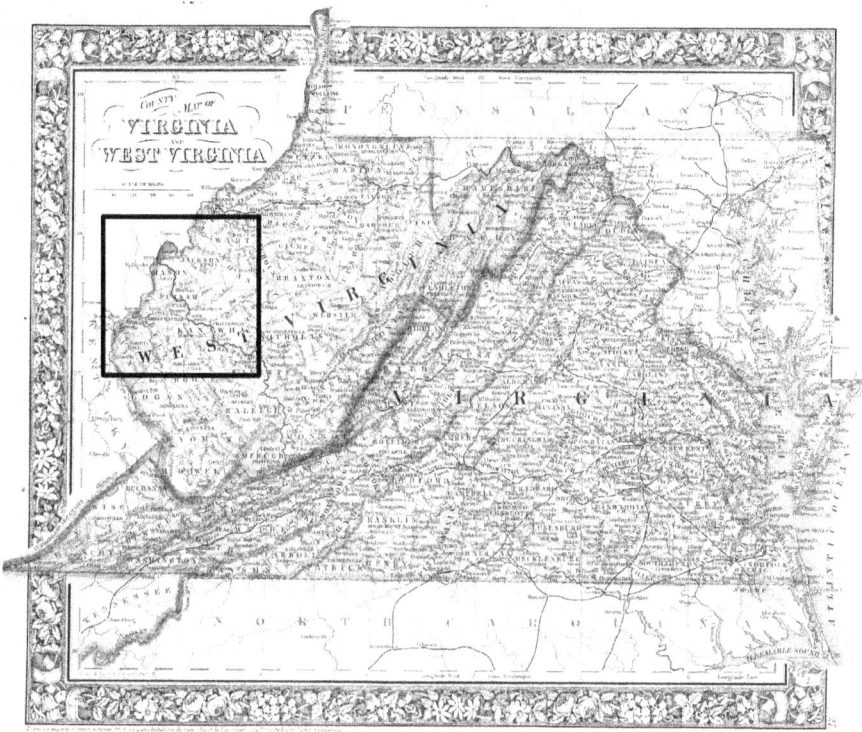

Source: County Map of Virginia and West Virginia. Mitchell, S.A. and Gamble, W.H., 1863. Philadelphia, PA. Courtesy Library of Virginia. View of Putnam County and surrounding region in the enclosed area. (also, see next page)

THE BATTLE OF HURRICANE BRIDGE, MARCH 28, 1863

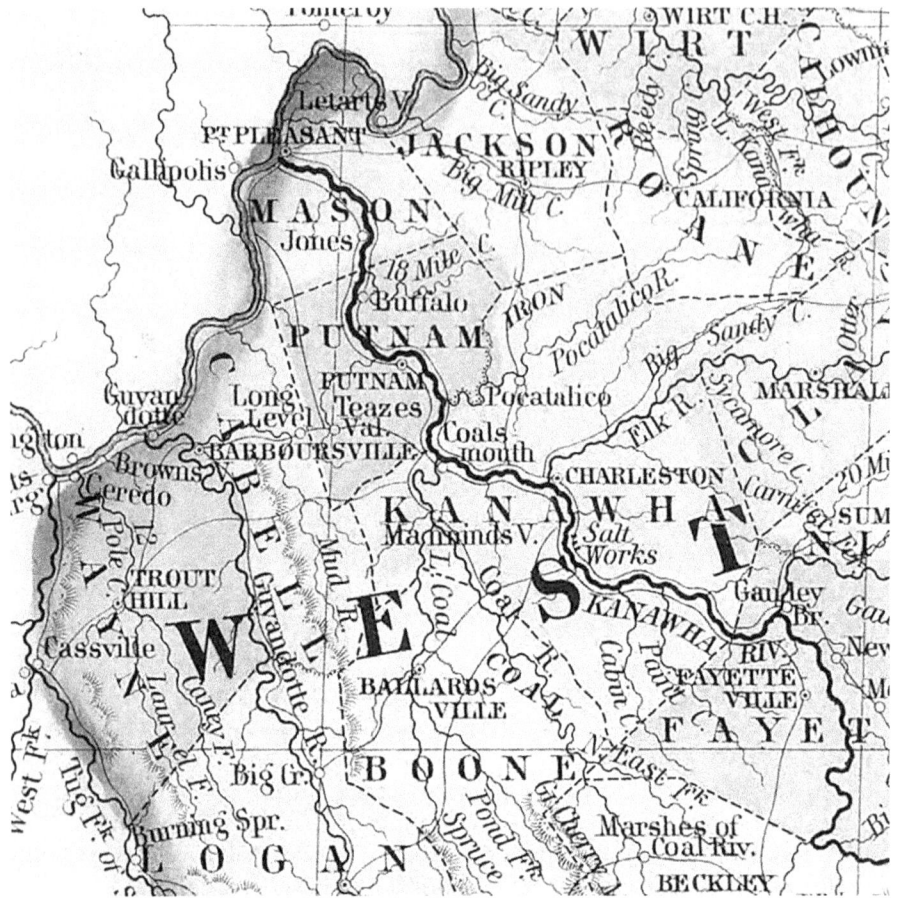

Enlarged view: Hurricane Bridge was located between Teazes (Teays) Valley and Long Level near the Putnam-Cabell County line.

INTRODUCTION

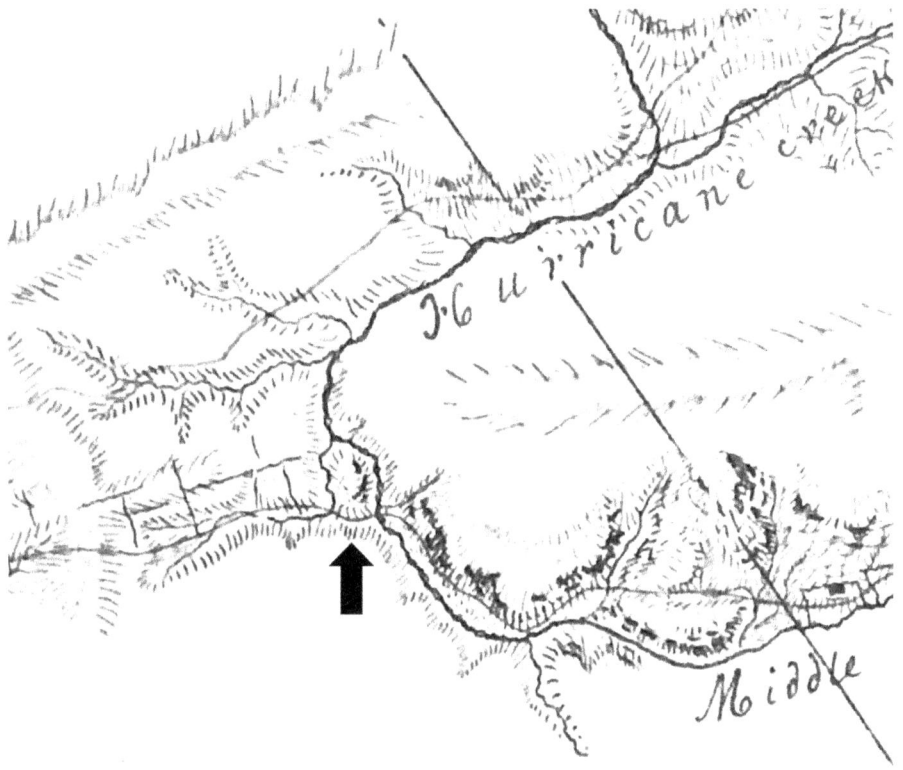

1829 Map Showing Extension of Kanawha Turnpike to the Mouth of the Big Sandy River. C. Crozet, Principal Engineer. Board of Public Works of Virginia, MS-754.3, R6, Part 2. Library of Virginia. Used with permission. View of Hurricane Bridge area showing the James River and Kanawha Turnpike route across Hurricane Creek (modern Harbor Lane). Arrow indicates the western heights area involved in the March 28, 1863, battle.

THE BATTLE OF HURRICANE BRIDGE, MARCH 28, 1863

Introduction References

1. Edens, Martin Van Buren. Battle of Hurricane Bridge! Poem published in *The Weekly Register*, April 30, 1863, Vol. 2(1), 1. Chronicling America, Library of Congress. (Hereafter Edens) Edens served in Company A, 13th West Virginia Volunteer Infantry and was present at the March 28, 1863 battle at Hurricane Bridge; Miller, O.R. Skirmish at Hurricane Bridge. 1996. *Hurricane Breeze*, Vol. 25, March 25, 1998, 1. (Hereafter Miller, Skirmish at Hurricane Bridge)

2. Shanklin, Harry L. *History of Putnam County*. 1967. Charleston, WV: Upper Vandalia Historical Society. (Hereafter Shanklin) Hurricane Centennial Committee. *Centennial History of Hurricane, WV: A History of Hurricane 100 Years, 1888-1988*. (Salem, WV: Walsworth Press, 1988) 6; 197. (Hereafter Hurricane Centennial)

3. Ibid., *Hurricane Centennial*.

4. Weiss, C.M.; Weiss, V.W.; Collins, R.L. "Revised Phase – 1 Archeological Survey of the Proposed Hurricane Bridge Park, Putnam County, WV." (December 2017). Manuscript prepared for City of Hurricane. Fairmont, WV: Allstar Ecology, LLC, 39-42; 51- 59; 63-65; 73-77; (Hereafter Weiss, et al, Archeological Survey); Griffith, Joe. *History of Company G, 11th West Virginia Volunteer Infantry: From Coalsmouth to Richmond, 1861-1865*. (Marietta, GA: Self-published Monograph, 1994), 69-70. (Hereafter Griffith)

5. *Hurricane Centennial*, 6; 197; Griffith, 69-70.

6. *Hurricane Centennial*, 195.

7. Shanklin; Griffith, 70; Personal interview by the author with Mrs. S. Duke, Culloden WV, February 15, 2019; Comstock, Jim. *Hardesty's History of Early West Virginia: Monroe, Putnam, and Tyler Counties*. (Richwood, WV: Privately published, 1973), 138-142. (Hereafter Comstock)

CHAPTER ONE

THE KANAWHA VALLEY DURING THE CIVIL WAR

P utnam County, West Virginia, was formed in 1848 from Cabell and Kanawha Counties, Virginia. When the Civil War began in April 1861, citizens of both Union and Southern sympathies quickly responded to the call to arms. A resident of Putnam County wrote, "No sooner did it become evident that the storm of war was about to burst like a might storm over this land, than the mustering of troops began in Putnam County Virginia, now West Virginia. Hundreds of her sons enrolled their names and shouldered arms in defense of their country."

Even with hundreds of men volunteering to serve in the Federal and Confederate armies from the region, citizens who remained at home faced a plethora of danger as the troops were not always available to protect them; at other times, their home area was under martial law by whichever army happened to be in control of the Kanawha Valley, and those on both sides faced harassment, imprisonment and, in some instances, murder. Any notion that the Civil War in western Virginia was less malevolent and bitter than in other parts of the country is quickly dismissed by numerous eyewitness accounts demonstrating how personal and violent the Civil War was in that region.[1]

From the outset of the war, near daily raids by Confederate guerillas were common place for Union citizens in the Kanawha Valley. During periods of Confederate occupation in 1861 and 1862, the military forces also routinely prowled, harassed and arrested Unionists. Conversely, those with Southern loyalties faced similar treatment from Union military and Citizen Patrols alike throughout the Kanawha Valley. The latter groups were state-sanctioned para-military volunteer organizations intended to protect Union families and their property, although they also had legal arrest authority and could detain persons suspected of "Secession" activities as long as two years.

In early February 1863, an incident occurred at Hurricane Creek in Putnam County that terrorized local residents and epitomizes the nature of the Civil War in western Virginia. A group of Confederate guerillas went to the home of Calvary Gibson, a known Union man on Hurricane Creek and murdered him in front of his wife and children. The incident was reported by a member of the 5th West Virginia Infantry, who were scouting in the area at the time and learned of it the next day. The soldier wrote of the atrocity in the *Ironton Register* on March 26, 1863, as follows,

> Editor Register: Allow me the use of your columns to give to your readers an account of a two days scout on the waters of Guyandotte and Mud Rivers. Lieutenant Witcher's Cavalry (not Claw Hammer) left this camp at one o'clock P. M. on the 18th inst., and marched that day to Poor's Hill, a distance of 25 miles through a drenching rain. We encamped that night without supper in a barn and in our wet clothes. Next morning, we resumed our march and brought up in the Keaton settlement, a distance of 40 miles from camp. Here is the place that a few days ago a company of the 13th [West] Virginia was fired upon from the bushes in retaliation for which a house or two soon disappeared. Here we found that a horseman had lately passed; we followed the trail up a by-path and a short turn in the way brought us (six

in number, not including Lieutenant Witcher) upon a log house, at which were hitched four cavalry horses.

A charge was ordered, four men came hastily out, armed and equipped; after a slight resistance and the exchange of a half a dozen shots, they were captured… This proved to be a very important capture, as among the squad was the leader of the gang, Lieut. Keaton, a desperado, that has been annoying the citizens of this part of Virginia for twelve months past, and has eluded vigilance, heretofore of the military authorities. This same Keaton was engaged in the murder of Mr. Gibson, a citizen of Virginia, who lived on the waters of Hurricane. The facts of that atrocity as related by the Prosecuting Attorney, are about as follows: This Keaton and his gang came to the house in the night and shot three balls into the room where they supposed he was, which hit within three inches of his wife's head. He was in another room and the gang went around to the other side of the house and went into his room. As he was putting on his pants, he cried out "for God's sake don't murder me. They paid no heed to his entreaties but shot him in his left breast. He fell and they shot into him four times as he lay on the floor writhing in his blood. His little girl ran about screaming to her mother "they've killed Pa, they've shot Pa," and got in the way of this brute C. S. A. Lieut. Keaton, and he threw her into the fire… This happened about a month ago and is fresh in the memory of many…"[2]

In western Virginia, small battles and skirmishes were the order of the day; while there was nothing on the scale of major campaigns such as Antietam or Gettysburg, the hundreds of small fights taking place there were often quite brutal. A good example is found in the story of one of the more notorious Confederates prowling through western Virginia, thirty-seven-year-old Captain Hurston Spurlock of Wayne County, who mustered into Company H, 16th Virginia Cavalry on August 31, 1861.

A quiet farmer before the war, he quickly became known for ruthless attacks on Federal troops and Union citizens. Spurlock was captured at Falls Timber in Wayne County by the 7th West Virginia Cavalry on January 27, 1864. Taken to prison at Wheeling, West Virginia, he transferred to Camp Chase, Ohio on February 5, 1864, where he was described as a "Desperate Character: Reported to have shot a Lieutenant after he had surrendered." Although too late to have been the same officer, the latter illustrates the bitter nature of warfare in this region; such incidents certainly occurred. A Union lieutenant was killed on February 15, 1864, in Wayne County, while held prisoner by the 16th Virginia Cavalry under Colonel Milton J. Ferguson. 2nd Lieutenant Oliver W. Griswold, Company H, 13th West Virginia Infantry was earlier captured on February 7, 1864, along with the 9th Illinois Infantry Quartermaster, a Sergeant from the 9th West Virginia Infantry, and another officer from the 91st Ohio Infantry.

The incident occurred as follows: Early in the morning of February 15, 1864, the prisoners were asleep in camp along Twelve Pole Creek wrapped in gray blankets given to them by their Confederate captors. At 7:00 A.M., a detachment of the 14th Kentucky Infantry and 39th Kentucky Mounted Infantry attacked the camp and captured Colonel Ferguson and 41 of his men in a brief, but intense skirmish. 2nd Lieutenant Griswold and the other three prisoners were killed in the fight; Although not present during the fight, a detachment from the 13th West Virginia Infantry was nearby under Lieutenant Colonel James R. Hall. His official report states the prisoners were killed by friendly fire also; a letter Hall wrote to the *Wheeling Intelligencer* newspaper states the prisoners were killed by Federals because they could not recognize them wrapped in gray blankets. However, the *Ironton Register* newspaper blamed the Confederates for killing the prisoners and the affair became quite controversial, reflecting the generally tense state of affairs in the region throughout the war. Griswold was from New York and relocated to Wayne County before the war. While speculative, it is not a foregone conclusion the prisoners died by friendly fire, particularly since Captain Hurston Spurlock of the same Confederate regiment was said to have killed a prisoner. To say the least, Lieutenant Griswold was well-known for his strong Abolitionist views in Wayne County, and was unpopular with Southern supporters there, particularly among the many of the men in the 16th Virginia Cavalry who knew him well. Ironically, both Spurlock and Griswold fought at Hurricane Bridge.[3]

INTRODUCTION

Captain Hurston Spurlock, Co. H, 16th Virginia Cavalry.
Courtesy Fred Lambert Collection, Marshall University Special Collections.

2nd Lieutenant Oliver W. Griswold, Co. H, 13th West Virginia Infantry. West Virginia State Archives.

MARTIAL LAW

By 1862, citizens in the Kanawha Valley found it increasingly difficult to avoid contact with opposing military forces operating in the area. Eighteen-year-old Victoria Teays Hansford, lived at Coalsmouth in Kanawha County (modern St. Albans, WV). She kept a diary, detailing her wartime experiences, and described an incident occurring in April 1862 when a squad of Federal soldiers came to search her home for contraband; someone had informed the soldiers that she was hiding a Confederate flag in her home:

> "I was left entirely alone. It was a cold overcast day, and I was sitting by the fire reading some old Dixie letters I had spread out before me. I also had a small silk flag draped over the back of the chair they were on…I heard the gate slam and looking out I saw four Yankee soldiers armed to the teeth headed for the door. The orderly sergeant in front wore a sword, a red sash, pistols etc., behind him were three men with muskets and I only had time to thrust my letters into the fire. The flag…went into my bosom, all this within a matter of seconds. With my heart pounding and thumping so loud I could hear it, I put on a calm face and met them at the door. They did not knock as they were a low-down squad that had been sent out by the Home Guard to search for contraband articles. The sergeant said he had been told I had a Rebel Flag which they had come for…I looked him straight in the eye and said, 'If you can find one here you can have it. I also told him he was perfectly welcome to search the house.
>
> Finding me so willing for them to search left him standing abashed. I then told him it was not necessary to have brought many men with muskets, swords and pistols when there was only one woman in the house to contend with. He finally sat down, and I became more polite and entertaining. I told him that I did have some flags he was welcome to. 'Where are they?' he said, 'There,' I said pointing to a framed picture on the wall of all the presidents. There were four small stars and stripes in each corner, but he was so ignorant he had a hard time telling them from 'Stars and Bars.' He finally said if that was all I had I was welcome to keep it. So I bowed them out very dignified, while my little treasure still lay close to my heart. This taught me a lesson to be always alert and never get caught napping…If those four men had been turned loose to search the house I would have lost valuable articles and perhaps been arrested. Our town was under martial law, and we were entirely under their power. We learned to be very discrete but also learned to be cunning."[4]

Although the Kanawha Valley was under Federal control, Confederate guerilla parties continued to conduct frequent nocturnal raids against Union families. This caused many citizens on both sides to assist troops in their efforts to oust the opposing forces from their home, by acting as spies and insurgents. Victoria Teays Hansford also indicated the Union soldiers also often questioned to the local slaves, in an effort to gain information of the Confederates' activities: "The Yankees were always interrogating the Negroes. Most of them were true and steadfast, but a few would let out little things that could get us in trouble. However, our colored people never in any way caused the Yanks to bother us, as long as they were with us."[5]

One of Victoria Hansford's contemporaries, nineteen-year-old Sarah Francis Young, lived on the eastern base of Coal Mountain in Putnam County, not far from Coalsmouth. She too kept a detailed diary. Her father, Captain John V. Young, served in Company G, 13th West Virginia Infantry and he was often away from home. Sarah was in a state of constant hypervigilance watching for Confederate raiders, with only her mother and two younger siblings at home. A party of Confederate guerillas led by Captain James Nounnan of the 16th Virginia Cavalry paid them a visit on the evening of September 12, 1862, just one night prior to the Battle of Charleston, when Confederate forces numbering 6,000 troops under Major General William Loring drove occupying Federal troops out of the Kanawha Valley. Captain Nounnan was looking for her father, who had gained a fearsome reputation among Southern citizens for his rough treatment to those whom he considered traitors. Captain Young and some of his men stopped by earlier that evening to rest, and Southern leaning neighbors had informed the Confederates that he was at home. Sarah Young described the incident as follows:

> They had been there but a short time before the men became sleepy, and Pa told them he would watch if they wished to sleep a little while. They all laid on the floor and I thought Pa looked tired. Emilie and myself told him we would watch if he wanted to rest. He laid down and in the course of an hour we heard horses coming. We wakened Pa directly, and he and the men ran out though the back door, passed around the corner of the house, but seeing too many Rebels to attack they slipped down the hill

back of the house into a ravine thickly set with alders. Two of the men ran on. One concealed himself along the fence to get a shot at them. Pa hid in a large bunch of alders. When the rogues stopped they found the horses tied, and asked us, very authoritatively, what those horses were doing here. Ma told them, as they answered her when she spoke to them, that it was an unfair question, and she would not tell them. I never in my life experienced such a time.

They stayed around the house about two hours, scouting through the yard and listening; no doubt expecting Pa to come after their horses. I never felt so much like abusing men in my life. One rough, ill-bred fellow would not tell me his name. I suppose he was ashamed of it. Burns, one of the set, told Ma his name was Dotson from Guyandotte. All the time they were here they would not move the horses. They were fastened in the back yard, and I reckon they thought Pa would come after them. While Pa was in the alder bush, a large, over-grown horse-thief came sneaking around him, and would stand listening within about ten steps of Pa. Pa said he fixed to shoot him, but he heard some more talking, and he thought he had better not. They came to the house, and we talked with them some. Indeed, my heart ached so I could scarcely talk. Old Dotson said he thought he could get married somewhere on this road. I told him Rebel beaux could not shine with the Union girl, but Yankees went like hot cakes. He said, 'I think I could make a Secesh out of you.' I gave him to understand quite different. He said something about 'homespun Yankees.' I told him they were home-spun Rebels. He said, 'I would like to stay about a week and quarrel with you.' After a while, the notorious horse thief, and blood-thirsty Rebel, Jim Nounnan, came along and called for a candle to search the house.

Emilie carried the candle and helped to search, laughing all the time at them. I told Nounnan I would not tell him who came here, and if I knew where they were I would not tell him. He said it was immaterial to him that he only asked for information here. I think he was mad, but I did not care. Dotson told us we would have to go to the North with our sweethearts or submit to Jeff

Davis. I hope he may never live to see the time. Well, I suppose they got tired of searching and waiting,. They bade us goodnight, wishing us good luck. Em [Emily] told them when gentlemen called on us we wanted them to come at a fashionable hour and not scare us half to death in the night. I told them I was not glad to see them and did not wish them good luck at all. And I don't." Sarah again observed on September 13, 1862 "The same evening the evening the Rebels were here, the Federal Cavalry came through Hurricane Bridge and captured six of their men. Good. They had no business here..."[6]

As such, the Civil War in the Kanawha Valley was very much a fratricide; former neighbors, co-workers, friends and even families were strongly divided on the political issues of the day. In many instances, the divisions took deep roots, and according to recent research, they were never fully reconciled. For example, one scholar recently noted the sectionalist division in Cabell County was so strong that it endured into the 20th Century. This was presumably related to a cultural "identity crisis" resulting from failure of both sides during Reconstruction to fully address the issues that caused the war to begin with, in spite of appearing to cooperate with the government's reconstruction efforts. The nature of warfare in western Virginia did not involve large battles with thousands of troops; the few battles occurring in the region typically involved far less than three thousand troops combined. Rather, the war in the Kanawha Valley was very focused and often personal, typically involving guerilla or partisan raids on specific families, known to stand for one side or the other.[7]

Federal troops in the area struggled to protect the Union citizens, however, as well as themselves from frequent Confederate raids, by both guerilla and military forces, which often occurred. During periods of Confederate occupation in the Kanawha Valley in 1861 and 1862 alike, dozens of Union citizens were arrested and taken to prison; a similar phenomenon occurred during periods of Union occupation against Southern leaning citizens. In some counties, local officials resigned due to the political upheaval and strife resulting from not only secession, but also from the issue of forming a new Union state from the Old Dominion, Virginia. Many places in western Virginia were left without civil authority in between periods of military occupation as a result, and in some places, things digressed into pure anarchy. To say the least, life as a civilian became extremely complex and unpredictable in this region of the country during the Civil War. Soldiers serving in the Federal units formed in western Virginia were also under constant strain fearing for their families' safety while they were off in the field.[8]

General Jacob Dolson Cox commanded Union forces in the Kanawha Valley during much of the 1862-1863 periods, and his headquarters were located in Marietta, Ohio. He had two field commanders immediately subordinate to him: Brigadier General George Crook, who commanded Union troops posted in the Gauley Bridge area, and Brigadier General Eliakim P. Scammon, whose headquarters were in Charleston, with outposts located at Point Pleasant, Hurricane Bridge, Barboursville, Coalsmouth (modern St. Albans) and Winfield. Scammon's troops were scattered along the James River Turnpike, Winfield and Coalsmouth, with division headquarters at Charleston, while Crook's troops, mostly Ohioans, were posted around the Gauley Bridge area, where his headquarters were located. On January 10, 1863, Cox had two divisions in the Kanawha Valley region, the First Kanawha under General Crook, and the Second Kanawha under General Scammon, totaling 14, 944 troops.[9]

Cox was born in Montreal, Quebec, Canada, in 1828. An insatiable student, he held interests in theology, education and law; he was admitted to the Ohio bar as an attorney in 1853. Cox was a strong Republican, with political aspirations. Elected to the state senate in 1859, he served until 1861. His political connections led to an appointment as a brigadier general of Ohio state militia in 1860, with no prior military background. He began diligently studying military tactics, military history and strategy when the war came, and raised hundreds of troops for the Union in 1861. This earned him a commission as a Brigadier General of Volunteers, and unlike many civilian appointees, Cox proved to be a very effective officer. Under his command, Federal troops in western Virginia maintained control of the Kanawha Valley from mid-1861. In August 1862, Brigadier General Cox received orders to take his five thousand troops of the Kanawha Division and join the Army of the Potomac in Maryland, as part of Major General Jesse Reno's Ninth Corps. He left Colonel James A.J. Lightburn in command of the remaining five thousand Union troops in the Kanawha Valley. Major General

Jesse Reno was killed at South Mountain on September 14, 1862, leaving Cox as the senior Brigadier General. He was given temporary command of the Ninth Corps under close supervision of Major General Ambrose Burnside, since he had no prior command experience at the corps level.

At the battle of Antietam on September 17, 1862, Cox advanced the 9th Corps on Robert E. Lee's right and nearly overwhelmed the Confederates late in the day, until General Ambrose P. Hill's Third Corps arrived to reinforce Lee, forcing Cox to withdraw. Antietam was afterward known as America's Bloodiest Day, with over 23,000 men killed, wounded or missing in action. President Abraham Lincoln was impressed with Cox's aggressive demeanor and recommended him to Congress for promotion to Major General, which was approved to rank from October 6, 1862. However, the promotion expired in March 1863, due to Congressional reports indicating there were too many general officers of that rank, and he was returned to the rank of Brigadier General until 1864, when he was re-commissioned as Major General. Cox and the Kanawha Division did not return to the Kanawha Valley until late October 1862, when he again assumed command of Union forces in the area.[10]

In spite of his military successes, General Cox was not altogether popular among citizens nor with Union soldiers who served under him in the Kanawha Valley. George C. Bowyer of Putnam County was one of those who disliked Cox. Raised the son of a wealthy slave-holder and former Sheriff of Greenbrier County, Bowyer owned a significant portion of land in Putnam and Kanawha Counties and was a slave holder himself. However, by May 1861 when he was elected to serve in the state legislature, Bowyer had become a strong advocate against slavery. He served as an *ex officio* member of the Restored Government of Virginia that met at Wheeling to organize the new state of West Virginia, and often corresponded with the new governor, Francis H. Pierpont, and other officials. On August 15, 1862, he wrote to Henry J. Samuels, the Adjutant General of the fledgling state, grousing about Cox's failure to provide sufficient military protection for Union citizens in Putnam County, pointing out Hurricane Bridge as a liability in particular:

> We have news of a fight at Chapmansville [Chapmanville] and that the Federals were retreating to Charleston - and were over

taken at Peytona & fighting there…We have had no troops at Hurricane Bridge for some weeks and if the Rebels drive our forces from Chapmansville we will have to yield in this section - Would it not be best to have a stronger force at the Mouth of Coal - also more troops at Hurricane Bridge, until we can get organised, and in a condition to take care of ourselves - if something is not done and that immediately we will have warm work in Putnam, which will disarrange all the plans for organization in this section. For my part I never could see why Genl. Cox remains at Flat Top Mountain killing horses and men getting supplies and doing no good - if he cannot get men enough to go on it does seem to me that he ought to fall back to Gauley where a forth of him men could hold the place and thereby save the trouble and expense of transporting supplies over rugged mountains - then the balance of his command could be stationed at various places in the Kanawha Valley in sufficient strength to defend themselves against the rebel cavalry prowling through the country This plan of putting a few companies in dangerous places - where reinforcements cant relieve them in time and where they are liable to be pounced upon and bagged by roving bands of guerrillas as in the case of Summersville & Chapmansville & other places - and keeping a heavy force at Flat Top or any other Top when they are doing no good, in perfect inactivity is not my idea of good Generalship."[11]

Jacob Dolson Cox. West Virginia State Archives.

Battle of Charleston September 13, 1862

With half of the Union forces removed from the Kanawha Valley, the remaining troop's capacity to repel a Confederate invasion was significantly weakened. Confederate Commander General Robert E. Lee saw this as an opportunity, and ordered Major General William Loring, a veteran of the Seminole Wars who lost his left arm in combat serving in Florida, to bring his six thousand Confederates and take control of the Kanawha Valley. Upon his departure, Cox turned over command to Colonel James A.J. Lightburn of the 4th West Virginia Infantry, whose headquarters were located at the Union garrison at Point Pleasant. On

September 13, 1862 Loring arrived at Charleston in Kanawha County and engaged Lightburn's five thousand Union troops. Fighting through the streets throughout the afternoon, heavy artillery bombardments from Union and Confederate batteries located along the Kanawha River created a cauldron of fire for both military and civilians, as hundreds attempted to evacuate.

The firing resulted in a great deal of damage to homes and businesses. Around 5:00 p.m., Lightburn ordered a retreat and burned several buildings, including a large supply depot, to prevent the Confederates from gaining access to them, resulting in over one million dollars in Union military stores lost. Union troops rapidly marched some fifty miles to Point Pleasant, with near constant harassment from Confederates and bushwhackers in pursuit. Bushwhackers were a type of partisan military organization, usually from the locality in which they operated, who harbored Confederate sentiments but were not actually enlisted or paid by the Confederate government. They were aggressive and used covert tactics to ambush and harass the large Federal columns typically moving about the area.

Confederate Guerillas. Woodcarving from Harper's Weekly, July 20, 1861. West Virginia State Archives.

THE BATTLE OF HURRICANE BRIDGE, MARCH 28, 1863

General Cox did not return to the Kanawha Valley until late October 1862; once General Loring established control of Charleston, the Confederates then held the Kanawha Valley for about six weeks, and the usual patrols and arresting Union citizens. Meanwhile, Federal authorities mustered a large force at Point Pleasant with intent to retake the valley. Once he had regained command, Cox assembled a force of some twenty-thousand men, mostly troops from West Virginia, Ohio, Illinois, Indiana and Tennessee, and marched toward Charleston in early November, with plans to drive the Confederates out, who were daily harassing Union citizens. Once General Loring realized the size of the force massed against him, he retreated south toward Dublin, Virginia without putting up a fight. Once more, the Federal army had control of the Kanawha Valley.[12]

The Kanawha Valley was again under martial law, yet General Cox faced increasing pressure to protect Union citizens in the area from raiding Confederates. Most of the guerillas and smaller military forces involved were, for the most part, from the Kanawha Valley region, including a Cavalry battalion commanded by Brigadier General Albert Gallatin Jenkins of Green Bottom in Cabell County. Jenkins formerly served in the United States Congress, was a wealthy planter with more than thirty slaves and a Harvard Law graduate. He commanded a battalion comprised of the 8th Virginia Cavalry and 16th Virginia Cavalry, who frequently raided and patrolled in the area. By all accounts, Jenkins did not bother to slow down his operations, even though General Loring was gone from the area.

Prominent citizens also frequently petitioned Francis H. Pierpont, the Governor of the Reformed Government of Virginia, for help protecting them, who in turn nudged Cox to act. This organization was formed in late April 1861 by elected representatives from the fifty counties of western Virginia who were opposed to, and voted against, secession at the Secession Convention on April 17, 1861, two days before Virginia seceded from the Union. Although a fledgling organization, the Union-minded officials quickly organized into a new state government and drafted a constitution, which gained President Abraham Lincoln's immediate support. By 1863, Lincoln was deeply involved in grappling with the issue of whether admitting the new state of West Virginia, by dividing the western counties of Virginia from those counties east of the Allegheny Mountains, was consistent with the U.S. Constitution. By March 1863, he was very close to formally admitting the new state into the Union.[13]

In late October 1862, General Cox was determined to re-establish communication with Union garrisons located at Barboursville in Cabell County and Ceredo in Wayne County via the James River and Kanawha Turnpike. This opened supply lines, and Union troops again maintained regular patrols operating through the area. Rumors abounded that the government would soon begin conscription, i.e. a military draft. Twenty-one-year-old Private David Burrows, Company F, 13th West Virginia, was stationed at Point Pleasant. He wrote to his wife on November 9, 1862, describing a recent scouting mission he went on covering over forty miles into Putnam County.

Burrows said they passed through Hurricane Bridge, where the soldiers interacted with several local citizens, "We was out to Hurricane, and it was a hard trip. There is a very hard talk down here of conscription, and I would like to know what people think about it here." Just four days previous, Burrows witnessed several friends with "heavy hearts" enlist in the 9th West Virginia Volunteers in his hometown of Gallipolis Ohio; this promoted him to think he needed to do his part also, and he enlisted in the 13th West Virginia Infantry on September 9, 1862 at Point Pleasant. He served in the Shenandoah Valley Campaign of 1864, where he became ill with Typhoid, and died at Cumberland Hospital in Maryland, on August 6, 1864.[14]

On October 30th, 1862, General Jacob D. Cox ordered a large expedition of Union troops in the Guyandotte and Barboursville area to re-open communication with Charleston following the recent Confederate withdrawal from the area. Cox's orders directed them to move toward Hurricane Bridge "scouting for Rebels who may be lingering in Putnam County." One of those soldiers was Private Samuel Huddleston of the 84th Indiana Volunteer Infantry, who wrote that Hurricane Bridge "…bore the marks of war. The bare chimney – monuments standing over the ashes of once peaceful and happy homes – and the absence of all able-bodied men told the sad story of a town which was one of the first to reap the bitter fruits of war. And this was only a sample of towns among the Western Virginia hills." One of those homes was likely that of twenty-eight-year-old Amazetta Thompson, who lived with her parents, Robert Napoleon Bonaparte and Julia Anne Morris Thompson at Hurricane Bridge. Their home had been burned by Union troops from the 34th Ohio Volunteer Infantry earlier in 1862, forcing them to relocate.[15]

Francis H. Pierpont. West Virginia State Archives.

Horse Thieves and Soldier Antics

On November 10, 1862, General Cox ordered Lieutenant Colonel James R. Hall, an alumnus of the Virginia Military Institute, to take four companies of the 13th West Virginia Infantry from Point Pleasant in Mason County, Virginia, and establish a garrison camp at Winfield in Putnam County to protect Union citizens there from guerilla raids. He took Companies A, B, D and G of the 13th West Virginia and set up a permanent camp site along the southern bank of the Kanawha River. Companies C, E and F of the 13th West Virginia remained at Point Pleasant. There were numerous Southern sympathizers in the area, and they were not pleased to learn that some three hundred Union soldiers were now encamped in their midst. As Cox busily contemplated solutions for protecting the Union citizens in the Kanawha Valley, as well as making plans to keep crucial supply lines open from Charleston into Putnam and Cabell Counties, he wrote on December 23, 1862 that he was dealing not only with harassment from Confederate cavalrymen roaming the region, but also guerillas, and in particular, angry Southern supporters who constantly accused Union soldiers of stealing horses, and other animals, and harassing their families.

Some of the accusations turned out to be true, as in the instance when a large group of angry citizens complained to Union officials at Winfield about one of the soldiers from the 13th West Virginia, who ingeniously created a scam to forage for food. He was going about the area telling local citizens he heard the Confederates were coming in large force, intending to create a panic, inducing them to evacuate their farms in order for him to poach their hogs, chickens, etc. When the angry mob approached Lieutenant Colonel Hall, commanding the post at Winfield, he thought there may be some truth to the notion the Confederates were lurking nearby and immediately sent out a cavalry detachment scouting for them. When it turned out to be a ruse, the guilty soldier confessed, and he was punished by being forced to carry a large load of bricks on his back during a series of dress parades, ordered for the battalion, lasting several hours for the next few days. His peers were fuming about having to march all day, but according to the veterans who saw it, they received more ire from officers for laughing at the soldier responsible than he took for creating the mess.[16]

Citizens of Hurricane Bridge were becoming increasingly afraid and concerned for their safety and that of their property due to constant raids and harassment from Confederates. Many supported Governor Francis Pierpont's election in 1861, and men from the village were serving in the Union army. Pierpont received several letters from residents asking him to protect them by placing Union troops there. He wrote to General Jacob Cox on December 4, 1862,

THE BATTLE OF HURRICANE BRIDGE, MARCH 28, 1863

The people in the vicinity of Hurricane Bridge have made a strong appeal to me to make an effort on their behalf to have troops placed in that vicinity; [General John] Floyd and Clarkson have troops behind them, and nothing is to prevent them from making raids in that direction. There are some troops at Winfield but a man or property may be seized within three miles of them and carried off before troops could get to their relief – they represent that a force there at Hurricane Bridge would gain a large section on the Kanawha River and also on the Ohio – they propose to give the benefit of their teams for hauling provisions if necessary. If there is a want of teams it is only 12 miles and a good turnpike road from Coalsmouth to Hurricane Bridge. I feel anxious on this matter as these people have contributed liberally in men and money to support the government and that they should be supported and protected. They ran to Ohio with the effects when Loring came in and now they want to protect their property. They have sent for 31 guns and ammunition which I have sent them showing their willingness to help...I learn there are four companies of the 13 Va [West Virginia] at Winfield. I would suggest the propriety of placing these companies at Hurricane Bridge which would protect both places-there is no danger at Winfield with Hurricane Bridge protected. [17]

Cox responded by turning the matter over to Brigadier General George Crook, who commanded the 1st Kanawha Division and was responsible for Union troops in the Kanawha Valley. Crook wrote to Pierpont on December 23, 1862, "I have the honor to inform you that I have this day ordered an expedition to Hurricane Bridge to remain there until further notice." Meanwhile, General Cox was becoming thoroughly annoyed with citizens constantly complaining and accusing his officers of stealing horses or other property. He received a letter from one of his subordinate officers, Captain Robert P. Kennedy, on December 22, 1862 informing him that another irate citizen, who was the local tax collector, had complained on December 11, 1862, that one of the locals requested he waive taxes on an animal that was allegedly stolen by one of the Union officers, Captain John Young of Coalsmouth, who commanded Company G of the 13th West Virginia. The citizen griped that Young had "pressed the animal" into Federal service without paying for it. Captain Kennedy wrote, "The pony claimed by Mrs. Thompson was found in his possession. The pony is returned to its proper owner.

This pony was taken…previous to his connection with the 13th Regt. Capt. Young has been placed in very peculiar circumstances ever since his entry into the service, his command has most always been right in the midst of inveterate enemies. He has lost by these enemies I believe all of his horses and was in the service some nine months, If I mistake not, has received as yet nothing for his services. He is a brave man, a good Captain, and uncompromisingly for the Union, and hates Secessionists intensely-has showed them little clemency. The consequence is they are trying to hunt him down. I make these remarks simply because I feel for the man, and do not want his character destroyed through the influence of those who hate him only because he tries to do them justice."

Cox responded to the complaint on December 23, 1862, "I have the honor to acknowledge the receipt of your letter covering inclosure from Mr. D.S. Montague, of December 11, 1862. I have referred the matter to Brigadier-General Crook, commanding in the Kanawha Valley. Means have already been taken to prevent the incursions of guerillas from the region of the Upper Sandy, and I hope there will be no more trouble from them. Mr. Montague's wholesale assertion that Union men in the valley have "no more favors shown them than the meanest dogs" deprives the rest of his communication of reliability, as, if he knows anything of the matter, he knows he is making a misstatement, and it is quite probable that he is trying to cover up his neglect of duty in his department by such abuse of military officers. Any specific complaints will meet with prompt investigation.

The troops stationed at Winfield are part of the 13th Virginia Volunteers, and I desire that you will require Mr. Montague to report at once whether he complains of them or of the general officers in command in the valley, giving full and specific details of the ground of his complaint, informing him that he will be expected to make good the charges, or be held responsible for a malicious effort to make trouble between civil and military authorities in West Virginia." Young defended himself by showing how he had no less than two horses stolen from his own farm by local Confederate guerillas, and that the government failed to provide him with a replacement mount, to which he was entitled as a captain. General Crook thought formal charges ought to have been brought against Captain Young when he learned of the matter, but the matter was eventually dropped. General Cox washed his hands of the matter, and returned to the task at hand, writing on December 22, 1862, "...I had also under consideration the feasibility of putting a force at Hurricane Bridge, but the lack of wagon transportation had so far deterred me from it. I have, however, referred the matter to General [George] Crook, with instructions to take such steps in this as may now seem practicable and to omit no precaution to give the people of that region full protection."[18]

Captain Young recruited men for his company in 1861 around the Coalsmouth and Putnam County areas. They initially served as a Citizen Patrol group, going around at night watching for Confederate raiders and protecting Union citizens. Following the large Union retreat from the Kanawha Valley after the Battle of Charleston on September 13, 1862, Captain Young's Company G was attached to the 13th West Virginia Infantry while at Point Pleasant; however, just prior to evacuating the Kanawha Valley, on or about September 11, 1862, Company G was involved in a brief skirmish near Hurricane Bridge.

Details are sketchy, although it is believed that the company was patrolling in Cabell County and encountered Confederates who fled from Guyandotte, and once caught up, engaged in a small skirmish with them near there. Company G remained at Winfield until January 28, 1863, when they were ordered to Coalsmouth, and Captain Young command the Union garrison there. Coalsmouth had several Union citizens, although it was known as a largely Secessionist area comprised of about fifteen hundred locals. Young faced several similar accusations from Southern citizens in that community again during their encampment there, until April 28, 1863; although Union officials gave serious consideration to such complaints about him or his men afterward.[19]

Lieutenant Colonel James R. Hall, 13th West Virginia Volunteer Infantry. West Virginia State Archives.

Captain John Valley Young, Co. G, 13th West Virginia
Volunteer Infantry. Co. G transferred into the 11th West Virginia Volunteer
Infantry in March 1864. Circa 1865. West Virginia State Archives.

CHAPTER ONE REFERENCES

1. Conner, Fred. "The Part Taken by Putnam Co. W.Va. During the War 1861-65 by Fred Conner, faithful servant of the 36th Virginia Infantry." Civil War Manuscripts, MS 79-18, No. 6, WV State Archives, 1-3. (Hereafter Conner)

2. WV AG Papers, Union Regiments 1861-1865, AR 383; Box 36; Broadsides and Oversized Items, No. 3. House Bill No. 5 Broadside, June 1861. WV State Archives; Capehart, Stephen P. Coalsmouth, *West Virginia Historical Magazine*, (1905), Vol. 5(1), 66-71; Turk, David S. *The Union Hole: Unionist Activity and Local Conflict in Western Virginia.* (Bowie, MD: Heritage Books, 1995), xxi, 9, 14, 21; *Official Records of the War of the Rebellion*, Series 1, Vol. 2, 195-196; (Hereafter OR) Sutherland, Daniel E. *A Savage Conflict.* (Kent, OH: Kent State University Press, 2013), 416-433; Curry, R.O. & Ham, Gerald; "The Bushwhacker's War: Insurgency and Counter-Insurgency in West Virginia." *Civil War History Journal*, Vol. 10(4), (December 1964), 86-91.; *Ironton Register* March 26, 1863, Vol. 13(70). Newspaper Reading Room, SN 84028882. Library of Congress.

3. Compiled Service Records, Record Group 94, M324, roll 148; CSR, Union Regiments, 13th West Virginia Infantry, RG 94, M508, Roll 206, National Archives (Hereafter CSR); Dickinson, Jack L. *Wayne County, West Virginia in the Civil War.* (Salem, Massachusetts: Higginson Book Company, 2003) 35-36; 64-65. (Hereafter Dickinson, Wayne County); OR Supplement, Vol. 3, Part 3, 317; *Wheeling Daily Intelligencer*, February 25, 1864 and *Ironton Register*, February 25, 1864 cited in Dickinson, Wayne County, 103-104. Oliver Griswold was a Dry Goods Merchant in Wayne County prior to the Civil War; his business partner was Kellian VanResalear Whaley, Colonel of the 9th West Virginia Infantry and later a United States Congressman.

4. Diary of Victoria Hansford Teays, Boyd Stutler Collection, MS78-1, Series 1, No. 8, July 1861, WV State Archives.

5. Wintz, William. *Civil War Memoirs of two Rebel sisters.* (Pictorial Histories Publishing, Charleston WV, 1989), 25-26.

6. Diary of Sarah Francis Young 1861-1862. Sept. 12 & 13, 1862. Typescript. West Virginia Regional History Collection, Roy Bird Cook Collection, Call No. AM 1651, WVU Library. Morgantown, WV.

7. Nichols, Seth A. "Let us Bury and Forget: Civil War Memory and Identity in Cabell County, West Virginia, 1865-1915."(2016). Unpublished Master's Thesis, Marshall University. Marshall University Library, Huntington, WV, vii; 1-13.

8. Rice, Otis. *West Virginia: A History*. (Lexington, KY: University of Kentucky Press, 1994 Reprint), 135-136.
9. OR, Series 1, Vol. 21, Part 1, 964.
10. OR, Series 1, Vol. 21, Part 1, 964; Cox, Jacob D. *Military Reminisces, of the Civil War*, Vol. 1, April 1861-November 1863. (Great Britain: Hard Press Books, 2016), 114-115; 118-122. (Hereafter Cox, Military Reminisces)
11. *Wheeling Intelligencer* July 21, 1863. "House of Delegates: Sketches Personal, Political and Biographical." George C. Bowyer, Putnam County. M-91, Misc. Reels, Newspapers on Microfilm, WV State Archives; WV AG Papers, Union Militia, AR 373, Putnam County, Box 2, Folder 1. WV State Archives.
12. OR, Series 1, Vol. 19, Part 1, 423-427; 458-461; 1057-1090; Series 1, Vol. 12, Part 3, 430-431; Cook Roy Bird. "The Civil War Comes to Charleston." *West Virginia History*, Vol. 23(2), (January 1962), 153-167; Cox, *Military Reminisces*, Vol. 1, 114-115; 118-122; See also: Lowry, Terry. *The Battle of Charleston and the 1862 Kanawha Valley Campaign*. (Charleston, WV: 35th Star Publishing, 2016). (Hereafter Lowrey, Battle of Charleston)
13. Parker, Granville. "The Formation of the State of West Virginia." (Wellsburg: Glass & Son Publishers, 1871), 1-2. Squires, J. Duane. "Lincoln and West Virginia Statehood." *West Virginia History*, Vol. 24(4), (July 1963). http: www.wvarchives.gov (Hereafter Squires, 1963); Ambler, Charles H. *Francis H. Pierpont: Union War Governor and Father of West Virginia*. (Chapel Hill, North Carolina: University of North Carolina Press, 1937), 3-11; 16-23; 29-32; 34-41.
14. Roush, Herbert L., Sr. "If Thou Wilt Remember: A Historical Narrative. The story of David M. Burrows, Company F, 13th West Virginia Volunteer Infantry." Unpublished monograph, (Lowell, Michigan, 1995). Call No. 973.781 R863, WV State Archives. (Hereafter Roush); Compiled Service Records, Union Regiments, 13th West Virginia, Record Group 94, M508, Roll 204, National Archives, Washington DC. (Hereafter CSR)
15. Wintz, W.D. (Ed.). "Recollections & Reflections of Mollie Hansford, 1828-1900." (Charleston, West Virginia: Quincy Copy Services, 1979), 35; Huddleston, Samuel B. Papers 1843-1917. Rare Books and Manuscripts Collection, Folder S694. Indiana State Library, Indianapolis, IN. See also: A Civil War History of the 84th Indiana Regiment as Recorded by Samuel Huddleston. 2007. Transcribed by Sharon Ogzewalla. Cambridge City, IN: Indiana State Library.

16. Washington, Davis. *Camp-fire Chats of the Civil War: Being the incidents, adventure and way-side exploit of the bivouac and battlefield, as related by the Veteran soldiers themselves.* (Detroit, MI: W.H. Boothroyd and Co., 1886), 204-209.

17. Pierpont, Francis H. Governor's Office Executive Letter Book. June 19, 1861 to March 25, 1864. Accession No. 37226, Box 1. Special Collections Microfilm Reel 619. Library of Virginia. Letter from Pierpont to General J.D. Cox December 4, 1862 and from Brigadier General George Crook to Pierpont December 23, 1862. (Hereafter Pierpont Executive Letter Book)

18. CSR, 13th West Virginia, RG 94, M594, Roll 196, National Archives; WV AG Files, AR 383, 11th West Virginia Infantry, Boxes 1 & 2, Folder 42, Company G Muster In record for Captain John V. Young; OR, Series 1, Vol. 19, 857; 1905; OR Series 1, Vol. 21, Part 1, 880-881; 997.

19. WV Adjutant General Papers, AR 383, 11th West Virginia Infantry, Boxes 1 & 2, Folder 42, Company G Muster Roll; WV AG Papers, AR 654, Folder 10-11, Part 1, Field History of the 13th West Virginia Volunteer Infantry. WV State Archives. (Hereafter 13th WV Field History); Civil War Letters of Captain John Valley Young, Company G, 11th West Virginia Infantry. West Virginia Regional History Collection, Call No. A&M 0895, Series 1, Correspondence, West Virginia University Library, Morgantown, West Virginia. (Hereafter J.V. Young Letters)

Chapter Two

Outpost at Hurricane Bridge

On January 22, 1863, General Jacob Cox gave one of his two immediate subordinates, Brigadier General Eliakim P. Scammon, command of the Kanawha District, and sent the other, Brigadier General George Crook, to take command of Union troops posted in the Gauley Bridge area. At that time, Cox's force was dispersed about the Kanawha Valley area as follows: the 5th West Virginia Infantry were posted at Ceredo, in Wayne County, and had detachments at Guyandotte. The 13th West Virginia Infantry had "half at Point Pleasant and half at Coalsmouth; at Charleston and Camp Piatt, each half a regiment."[1]

The 13th West Virginia was formed in September-October 1862 at Point Pleasant in Mason County, under command of Colonel William R. Brown, a Pennsylvania native. He was born October 11, 1823, and during his youth tended to drift through the western territories from Iowa to Kansas, with a strong interest in mechanics and metal alchemy. He eventually settled in Pomeroy, Ohio, where he became foreman of a brass foundry and machine shop. As the Civil War broke out, he recruited forty men from his foundry and went to Point Pleasant, Virginia, to join the Union army. There, they enlisted in the 4th West Virginia Volunteer

Infantry, and Brown was quickly elected their captain and assigned to Company E.

Brown proved to be a stern, but efficient, officer and was promoted to Colonel and given command of the 13th West Virginia Infantry on September 16, 1862. Brown commanded the regiment through the 1864 Shenandoah Valley Campaign, and at Petersburg, where on March 15, 1865, he was given a Brevet Promotion to Brigadier General. After the war, he relocated to Kansas City, Missouri, where he later served as a county commissioner and probate judge, and at the time of his death, he was a member of his county board of education. He died of pneumonia at home, aged 65 years, on Tuesday, March 24, 1891.[2]

During their time in the Kanawha Valley, companies of the 13th West Virginia were involved only in a few small skirmishes and raids, usually repelling bushwhackers or patrols seeking Confederate cavalry and guerillas prowling the region. Bushwhackers were local Confederate guerilla forces, which were intimately familiar with the rough, mountainous terrain and made frequent ambuscades, and other surprise attacks, on Union citizens and harassed military forces across the region. They also tangled with Confederate military forces during raids, patrols and other small conflicts. Even so, the regiment had yet to see a larger engagement as a singular unit. Captain James W. Johnson of Company A, 13th West Virginia Infantry, was the senior captain among the regiment's company commanders. He was at Winfield, with companies A, B, D and H under Lieutenant Colonel James R. Hall on February 10, when Hall received orders from Colonel Brown to establish an outpost at Hurricane Bridge. Hall ordered Johnson to take Companies A, B, D and H to Hurricane Bridge in Putnam County, where they arrived late in the afternoon that day, and immediately established an encampment. Note that several historians have supposed Company G of the 11th West Virginia was also present, but this is inaccurate.[3]

Upon arrival at Hurricane Bridge, Companies A, B, D and H under command of Captain Johnson immediately began constructing "a large earthen fort." This meant spending several hours per day digging large mounds of dirt with shovels and other implements. The soldiers were not pleased to follow this order, yet Colonel Brown later recalled, they "daily improved their earthworks" during February and March 1863, although the fort was yet unfinished at the time of the March 28 battle.

Their immediate objective was to guard access to the bridge spanning Hurricane Creek, and to control access to the James River Turnpike in that area. Another primary objective was to protect local Union citizens; Captain Johnson routinely sent out patrols into the village and nearby areas looking for Confederates. Often the patrols would march thirteen to fifteen miles per day, and covered areas west toward Barboursville, and northeast as far as modern Scott Depot. He also established daily picket posts guarding access to the fort along the turnpike and near the camp and hospital sites. The term "Pickets" was Civil War era military parlance for sentries; i.e. soldiers posted outside of a camp or other position to guard against unwanted surprise attacks, and also to provide an early warning system. Intended to delay and harass approaching troops by slowly and systematically falling back toward the main body of troops firing in sequence, pickets were typically placed in large, concentric circles or semi-circles at intervals of ten to fifteen yards apart, extending up to a half mile or longer if needed, dependent upon the location and circumstances.[4]

James William Johnson enlisted in the 13th West Virginia Infantry on August 15, 1862 at Coalsmouth, Virginia, at age twenty-four years, and was soon elected captain. He later tendered his resignation on May 15, 1863, and transferred to Company C, 3rd U.S. Colored Troops as a 1st Lieutenant on July 20, 1863 by Special Order No. 335 of the U.S. War Department. Interestingly, he told Colonel Brown prior to resigning that his reason for taking the new assignment was to accept a "higher position" of rank. Johnson was also later detailed as Brigade Inspector on September 20, 1863, and eventually promoted to captain on October 8, 1864, while stationed in Jacksonville, Florida, by Brigadier General E.K. Scammon, who was familiar with his service in western Virginia, as his former commander while in the Kanawha Division.[5]

Captain Milton Stewart commanded Company B. He originally enlisted at age nineteen years in the 4th West Virginia Infantry on August 20, 1862, at Point Pleasant. He was quickly promoted to the rank of sergeant, and soon afterward elected Captain in October 1862. At age twenty-one years, Stewart was wounded by gunshot to the left thigh at the battle of Winchester on September 19, 1864 and hospitalized at Cumberland Hospital. He remained there until deemed unfit for duty due to disability by Dr. C.D. Daley, regimental surgeon on

November 30, 1864, and was given leave of absence; however, Stewart did not agree, and returned to his regiment. Captain Stewart was promoted to Lieutenant Colonel on December 10, 1864 and re-assigned to duty at Department Headquarters by General Orders No. 1 in January 1865, where he served as Inspector General on Major General George Crook's staff until the end of the war.[6]

As a regiment, the 13th West Virginia had yet to face an enemy on an open battlefield as a cohesive fighting unit. Heretofore, their combat experience was largely by company during various patrols, scouting missions and disrupting guerilla operations. Private Jacob Shoemaker of Company D was "accidentally wounded in the hand" while cleaning a loaded rifle. This bears further testimony of the inexperienced troops first garrisoning Hurricane Bridge. Typical of volunteer regiments, there were also often internal conflicts affecting morale. Commanders were often inexperienced political appointees as well. Most recruited men from their home area, which typically led to indulging a great deal of leeway in dealing with their subordinates. In other words, strict adherence to military discipline by volunteer officers was rare in western Virginia. Colonel William Brown, who commanded the 13th West Virginia, however, was an exception. Although not a career army officer, Brown was known for his rigid, by the book discipline, and many soldiers dreaded having to deal directly with him.[7]

Colonel William R. Brown, 13th West Virginia Volunteer Infantry.
Terry Lowry Collection.

Captain James W. Johnson, Co. A, 13th West Virginia Volunteer Infantry. West Virginia State Archives.

Captain Milton Stewart, Co. B, 13th West Virginia Volunteer Infantry. West Virginia State Archives.

1st Lieutenant Lovell C. Rayburn, Co. B, 13th West Virginia Volunteer Infantry. West Virginia State Archives.

2nd Lieutenant Samuel S. Mathers, Co. A, 13th West Virginia Volunteer Infantry. US Army History Education Center.

2nd Lieutenant George Snowden, Co. D, 13th West Virginia Volunteer Infantry. Snowden was a Sergeant at the time of the March 28, 1863, Battle at Hurricane Bridge. West Virginia State Archives.

Unidentified Federal Officer of the 13th West Virginia Volunteer Infantry. West Virginia State Archives.

THE BATTLE OF HURRICANE BRIDGE, MARCH 28, 1863

Sergeant Robert H. Davis, Co. A, 13th West Virginia Volunteer Infantry. Post-war image. US Army History Education Center.

New Recruits and Deserters at Hurricane Bridge

While stationed at Hurricane Bridge, the 13th West Virginia also acquired three new recruits on March 1. Private William Hurel was from Kanawha County. He enlisted in Company A, and was 5'6" tall, with black eyes, dark hair, and fair complexion; he worked as a farmer prior to enlistment. Twenty-year-old Private Adam Roberts of Charleston also enlisted in Company B, and eighteen-year-old Philip Wintz, Jr., enlisted into Company A. The green recruits had but three weeks in service, with minimal training or discipline before they saw combat for the first time.

A fourth man enlisted in Company H there on February 24: Private Charles M. Dawson.[8]

From the period of February 10, 1863, to March 28, 1863, there were at least ten soldiers identified as Absent without Leave (AWOL) on morning reports and muster rolls who faced charges of desertion when caught. However, two men are known to have abandoned their post and took "French Leave," i.e. deserted, during the battle. Private John Carr of Company D survived the March 28, 1863 battle, and then deserted from Hurricane Bridge on June 28, 1863. Officers supposed he was hiding out in Pennsylvania; Carr never returned to the regiment. Others were not so fortunate; Private David Bailey of Company B was aged forty years and ironically survived the fight at Hurricane Bridge, only to be killed by a citizen in Mason County a few weeks later while on patrol on May 28, 1863. Two days after arriving at Hurricane Bridge on February 8, 1863, two men from company B were arrested and placed in confinement for attempting to desert. A third private from Company H also managed to desert, Private Dolison Workman, who was found to be AWOL shortly after arriving at Hurricane Bridge but returned on February 28, 1863.[9]

However, archival records often indicate a given soldier deserted, and then later shows they were captured, or in hospital, and in some instances, at home on authorized leave. Regimental Adjutants were typically the more administratively-minded officers, many having been successful businessmen or clerks prior to the war; however, human error and randomness of war must be given consideration before pejoratively concluding a soldier deserted, particularly when evidence is sparse, as it is known they often misplaced documents, or sometimes did not have time to complete lengthy forms. Many were also destroyed after the war.

A good example is that of thirty-four-year-old Private Nathan Burchfield of Company D who was originally from North Carolina. He fought in the March 28, 1863 battle, and was supposed to have afterward deserted, but was later found innocent. Burchfield was subject to suspicion by his comrades to begin with, having been raised in the South and enlisted in a Federal unit. He was marked as a deserter on October 14, 1863 but testified at his December 1864 Court Martial that he was detached as an ambulance driver during the Shenandoah Valley Campaign and captured on September 4 and taken to Richmond on

September 22, 1864. Prisoner of War records indicate he was paroled on September 22, 1864, at Aiken's Landing, and given a pass to return to his regiment. Somehow, he ended up enroute to a hospital at Chambersburg, Pennsylvania, when he was arrested by a detective on October 3, 1864. Burchfield testified, "My pass was torn up by him and I was turned over to the Provost Marshall." Charges were dropped, and Burchfield served until the end of the war.[10]

Colonel William Brown was not only a staunch stoic, but he was also quite pragmatic, often to the degree that it resulted in his men perceiving him as calloused and unfair. Regardless, he tended to make decisions based on unit necessity, rather than individual welfare, an important trait for any field commander. An example of the latter was Captain Taylor W. Hampton, who commanded Company H. He resigned on February 26, 1863, roughly one month before the battle. He told Colonel Brown that his wife and children all had taken severe illnesses, causing him "much trouble and anxiety," rendering him unable to fulfil his duties. Hampton also requested that he be allowed to exit under honorable conditions, given he had served without impairment prior to that point. He had assumed command of the company on November 5, 1862, and was by all accounts an efficient officer, prior to the onset of his family circumstance.

Colonel Brown did not hesitate to approve his resignation and forwarded a letter to Major General B.F. Kelley on February 28, 1863, suggesting he receive anything but an honorable departure. He intimated to General Kelley that Hampton failed to properly manage his present difficulties, which had left him in "such a distracted frame of mind" that in his opinion, "the resignation would be of no harm to the service." It was accepted by Major General B.F. Kelly, who commanded Union forces in western Virginia, on March 10, 1863; however, Hampton died from an unspecified illness on March 9, 1863, before he could return home.[11]

Hampton's immediate subordinate, 1st Lieutenant Oliver W. Griswold, was given temporary command of Company H upon Hampton's death, and led the company during the March 28, 1863, battle. He was formally assigned command of Company H from November 4, 1863. Lieutenant Griswold seemed to attract dire circumstances; on February 7, 1864, he led a patrol into Wayne County from Guyandotte and was captured by Captain Milton Ferguson's Company of the 16th Virginia Cavalry – ironically one of the very same outfits he would fight on March 28. While a prisoner of war, Griswold was killed in early 1864, in the area "between the headwaters source at Lick Creek..."[12]

There are several inaccuracies published regarding the identity of Federal troops garrisoning Hurricane Bridge during February and March 1863. Fredrick "Fred" Conner, a former slave, was a resident of Buffalo in Putnam County prior to the Civil War. He kept detailed records of events transpiring in Putnam County, as well as activities of the 36th Virginia and other units from the area. In particular, he collected several post-war letters describing battles occurring at Scary Creek, Barboursville, Guyandotte and Hurricane Bridge. Unfortunately, there are also some inaccuracies in Conner's accounts that have misled researchers since the late 1800's.

This is a common issue with post-war recollections, because many were written several years following the war, and with the passing of time, certain details are easily lost or confused. For example, Conner summarized a letter written by Colonel James M. Corns, who later commanded the 8th Virginia Cavalry, and also documented several recollections of the battles of Scary Creek, Barboursville and Hurricane Bridge; however, he warned the reader to excuse him if some of his recollections did not seem right, noting "...I am now in my 80th year and nervous..." Conner also reported that Companies A, B, D and G of the 11th West Virginia Infantry were stationed at Hurricane Bridge during February – March 1863. However, while Company G later served in the 11th West Virginia, during 1863 that unit was still attached to the 13th West Virginia Infantry; although it was posted at Coalsmouth from January to April 1863 and not at Hurricane Bridge.

As Conner's records were one of the only primary sources known to historians in the post-war period, it was generally accepted at face value as being accurate. However, Conner's information is contradicted by evidence found in military records. This seemingly small, but significant, error led to decades of misinformation about who was stationed at Hurricane Bridge at the time of the March 28, 1863 battle.

Colonel William Brown left a brief, but detailed, field history of the regiment's activities from its formation until the close of the war. That document, along with other records, such as the personal letters and diary of Captain John Valley Young, who commanded Company G, consistently indicate that his Company G was attached to the 13th West Virginia Infantry from August 1862 through March 1864; at that time, they were transferred into the 11th West Virginia Infantry. However, from January to April 1863, Company G was stationed at Coalsmouth. On February 10, 1863, General Cox ordered a detachment of four companies from the 13th West Virginia Volunteer Infantry, A, B, D and H, who were then posted at Winfield in Putnam County, to establish an outpost at Hurricane Bridge.

These companies were previously posted at Point Pleasant until November 10, 1862, when Companies A, B, D, H and G under command of Lieutenant Colonel James R. Hall were sent to establish a garrison camp at Winfield in Putnam County. They remained there through February 10, 1863; however, on January 28, 1863, Company G, commanded by Captain John Valley Young of Putnam County, was ordered to Coalsmouth (modern St. Albans), and took command of the garrison camp there. Coalsmouth then had several Union citizens, although it was known as a largely Secessionist area comprised of about fifteen hundred locals. Companies C, E and F of the 13th West Virginia then remained at Point Pleasant.[13]

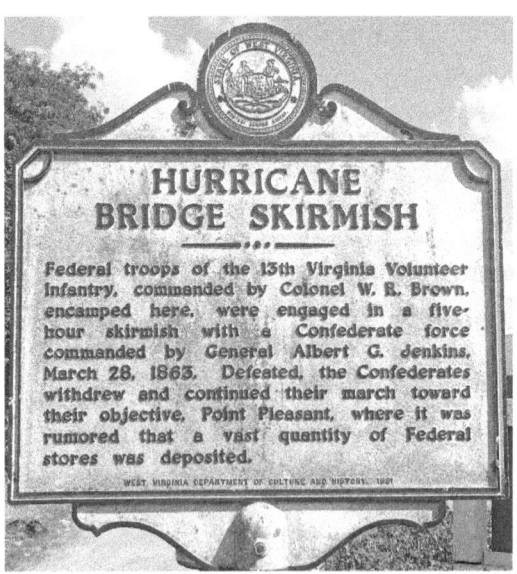

Hurricane Bridge state historical marker

Courtesy Hurricane Breeze Newspaper, February 19, 1998. Hurricane Bridge area showing the state historical marker and the bridge over Hurricane Creek. This part of the field was not used in the March 28, 1863, battle. The western heights are shown in the distance.

DEMOGRAPHICS

Many of the soldiers comprising the four companies garrisoning Hurricane Bridge on March 28, 1863, were local to Putnam, Mason, Wayne and Kanawha counties; a few were also from Meigs County, Ohio. There were exceptions, including Corporal Thomas M. Campbell of Company D. He was born in Northampton County, England, and thirty-four-year-old Private Nathan Burchfield of Company D was originally from North Carolina. There were five pairs of brothers who enlisted at the same time in the 13th West Virginia during 1862.

Two of those men were twenty-one-year-old Private James H. Gaskins of Company B, who enlisted with his younger brother, nineteen-year-old Samuel Gaskins in October 1862 at Point Pleasant; however, Samuel was assigned to Company F, and the other four pairs served in the same company. The majority of soldiers enlisting in the 13th West Virginia were farmers, and the average age at enlistment in 1862 was twenty-four years, seven months. (See Appendices B-E) There were six boys at age sixteen years in the ranks, Privates Abner Nunley and David Smith of Company A; Private Christopher Barnette of Company B (he died of Pneumonia in February 1863 just weeks prior to the battle); and also, Privates William B. Cherry; Lewis C. Johnson and John Taylor of Company D.[14]

Many Union soldiers and their families in western Virginia became refugees when they were driven away from their homes at gunpoint by Confederates in 1861-1862. They lived with constant reports from their families of harassment, and often harm, at the hands of Confederate raiders. As a result, there was little, if any, sense of fratricide felt by these Union soldiers, who were quick to give hostile reactions to Confederates, whether civilian or military. Most saw themselves as simply defending their homes from attack, which often involved the same Confederates facing them on March 28, 1863. Quite often, Union troops patrolling the Kanawha Valley were also engaged in similar operations against Southern citizens, typically arresting those known to agitate Secessionist sympathies, who were then sent off to Union prisons. Union troops in the region were under strict orders not to forage from civilians, although there are numerous accounts of soldiers accused of taking farm animals and horses from Southerners.[15]

An example still fresh in their memories was the November 10, 1861 raid on the Union garrison at Guyandotte in Cabell County, when the same Confederate troops led by General Jenkins conducted a surprise attack late Sunday evening and routed the 9th West Virginia Volunteer Infantry, capturing, killing or wounding most of the garrison. The most venomous sting of that raid for Union men in the area was the awareness that dozens of Southern minded citizens had aided Jenkins in executing the raid by sending intelligence on their strength, positions, etc. prior to the attack. The Confederates occupied the village, and on the next day, the 5th West Virginia arrived and attained vengeance; they burned several homes and businesses known to belong to Secessionists.

Private Samuel Gaskins, Co. E, 13th West Virginia Volunteer Infantry. Brother of Private James H. Gaskins, Co. B, 13th West Virginia Volunteer Infantry. Private collection, used with permission.

How many Union soldiers were at Hurricane Bridge?

It is commonly thought the number of Federal troops present at Hurricane Bridge on March 28, 1863, was one-hundred-fifty soldiers, based on the official report posted by Captain James Johnson, who commanded the garrison. He stated, "All available force numbering about one hundred and fifty effective men were drawn up inside our fortifications when the enemy appeared in force..." However, a review of muster rolls and morning reports for the 13th West Virginia Infantry from January to March 1863 showed a marked discrepancy in Captain

Johnson's report and the number of men actually reported as present on company records. For example, muster rolls from Companies A, B, D and H from March 1863 showed two hundred sixty-three soldiers had enlisted in those four companies.

The morning reports taken for each company at Hurricane Bridge on the morning of March 28, 1863, showed there were then two hundred twenty-seven enlisted men present, and eleven officers, totaling two hundred thirty-eight troops aggregate available for duty on the day of the battle. Eight other troops were assigned extra duties outside of the camp at that time (digging coal for fuel and chopping firewood), and four men were absent without leave. Morning reports from Company A also showed Captain Milton Stewart and ten men had just returned from a week-long scouting mission around Putnam County on March 26, but all were present on March 28.

According to the 13th West Virginia Field History, Companies C, E and F were stationed at Point Pleasant on March 28, 1863, and were not involved in the battle at Hurricane Bridge. Note that when word of the attack at Hurricane Bridge reached General B.F. Scammon's headquarters in Charleston, he ordered Companies C and F to march to Hurricane Bridge from Point Pleasant post haste to reinforce the garrison. Captain John D. Carter commanded Company E, and his account of the attack on the garrison at Point Pleasant was published in the Point Pleasant Weekly Register Newspaper on April 4, 1863. Captain Carter indicated he had only around sixty men available for duty on March 30 and said nothing of having a larger force comprised of men from Companies A, B, D and H present. Review of company records including morning reports, muster rolls and officer correspondence did not show evidence that any of those four companies were divided into detachments and sent elsewhere on March 28; therefore, the number of men reported present that date on morning reports is considered an accurate accounting of those present. (See Table 1)

Company records further showed there were seventy-four officers and enlisted men from the four companies reported as being home on sick leave or in the hospital during February and March, causing a dramatic reduction in Union troop strength. Another twenty-nine men were reported as present but sick on the morning of March 28, 1863. As there is no record of any of the latter twenty-nine men being quarantined or sent to the army hospital at Point Pleasant on that date, they are presumed to have fought in the battle while ill. Note that service records also showed most of the men reported sick at Hurricane Bridge during February-March 1863 had typhoid or pneumonia, and a few had both; as a result, the overall health of the regiment is considered poor on the date of the battle, which is also a significant factor in terms of their fighting efficiency.

Generally, morning reports were compiled by both company officers and senior non-commissioned officers on a daily basis, and therefore are reliable data regarding troop strength of a given military unit during the Civil War. This is because those data were collected daily and counter signed by the company First Sergeant, junior officers and company commander. Muster rolls, on the other hand, while still considered a reliable data source in most instances, were often compiled monthly or quarterly by company clerks using data from morning reports and initial muster rolls at the time of enlistment, and occasionally one finds certain information is missing or was inaccurately recorded when compared against morning reports and other records. As a result, such data must be carefully interpreted, given the possibilities for errors or omission.

For example, when men were in the hospital or home sick, or on detached service, muster rolls do not always notate it. Another common problem with records from West Virginia's Union regiments is that from 1861-1863, many men did not sign their muster sheets upon enlistment, and simply went into service with a given company. Many expressed concerns they did not want to put their names on official documents, for fears their families would suffer retaliation if the records were ever captured, or that they would be later forced to serve in theaters far from their homes in western Virginia in the event of a conscription (military draft).

The result was that a few men who may have served in a given organization are not found on muster rolls or morning reports at all, but in many instances their service can be documented by other sources such as hospital records, prison documents or soldier letters or diaries. This is important to grasp, because it appears the Union force was much larger than previously reported in nearly all previously published accounts of the affair, albeit it was significantly weakened by generally poor health in the four companies. It is unclear as to why Captain Johnson reported having only 150 men; however, his report was written just a few days after the battle, and there was much transpiring in the regiment at that time. He could have easily miscalculated the number of men present.[16]

Table 1
Union Troops at Hurricane Bridge March 28, 1863

Company	Officers	Enlisted	Detached Duty	Sick at Home-Hospital	Sick Call	Leave	AWOL
A	2	59	3	30	8	4	0
B	3	58	1	16	7	0	0
D	3	56	4	8	7	0	4
H	3	54	0	20	7	0	0*
Total	11	227	8	74	29	0	4

Notes: Two men from Company D returned to duty from the Field Hospital on March 29, 1863. Detached duties were usually digging coal and cutting firewood.
*One man from Company H returned from desertion on February 26, 1863.

Source: Records of the Adjutant General's Office (Record Group 94), Book Records of Union Organizations, 13th West Virginia Infantry, Vol. 4 of 4, Morning Reports, Companies A-D, F-K, March-February 1863. Accession No. E112-115, PI-17. National Archives, Washington DC.

CHAPTER TWO REFERENCES

1. OR, Series 1, Vol. 19, 857; 1905; OR Series 1, Vol. 21, Part 1, 880-881; 997.

2. CSR, 13th West Virginia, RG 94, M508, Roll 114, National Archives; WV AG Papers, Union Regiments, 4th and 13th West Virginia Infantry, AR 382, Boxes 12 & 23. WV State Archives; Miller, Richard F. (Ed.). *States at War: A Reference Guide to Ohio in the Civil War.* Vol. 5. Lebanon NH: University Press, 401; *South Kansas Tribune*, March 25, 1891; The Star and Kansan, Friday March 27, 1891.

3. 13th West Virginia Field History, Part 1; Griffith,5-12; Comstock, 131; Conner, 6-8.

4. Ibid., 13th West Virginia Field History.

5. CSR, 13th West Virginia Infantry, RG 94, M508, Roll 207, National Archives.

6. Ibid, M508, Roll 209.

7. Records of the Adjutant General's Office (Record Group 94), Book Records of Union Organizations, 13th West Virginia Infantry, Vol. 4 of 4, Morning Reports, Companies A-D, F-K, March-February 1863. Accession No. E112-115, PI-17. National Archives, Washington DC. (Hereafter 13th WV Morning Reports)

8. CSR, 13th West Virginia, RG 94, M508, Rolls 207; 209 and 210, National Archives; WV AG, Union Regiments, 13th West Virginia, AR 382, Box 20 Muster Roll April 10, 1863, WV State Archives; 13th West Virginia Morning Reports, February 24, 1863, Company H.

9. CSR, 13th West Virginia, RG 94, M508, Roll 204, National Archives; WV AG Papers, Union Regiments, 13th West Virginia, AR 382, Box 23, Companies B & D Muster Rolls. WV State Archives; 13th West Virginia Morning Reports, February 28, 1863, Company H.

10. CSR, 13th West Virginia, RG 94, M508, Roll 204, National Archives; WV AG Papers, Union Regiments, 13th West Virginia, AR 382, Boxes 20. WV State Archives.

11. CSR, 13th West Virginia, RG 94, M508, Roll 206, National Archives; WV AG Papers, Union Regiments, 13th West Virginia, AR 382, Box 20 Muster Roll April 10, 1863, WV State Archives.

12. Ibid.

13. Conner, 6-8; Miller, O.R. Skirmish at Hurricane Bridge, 1; Hurricane Centennial, 3-5; Comstock, 131; J.V. Young Letters 13th WV Field History, Part 1; OR, Series 1, Vol. 19, 1083.
14. CSR, 13th West Virginia, RG 94, M508, Rolls 204 & 206, National Archives; WV AG Papers, Union Regiments, 13th West Virginia, AR 382, Boxes 20. WV State Archives; See Appendix B-E also for demographic information.
15. Geiger, Joe. *The Civil War in Cabell County, West Virginia 1861-1865.* (Charleston, WV: Pictorial Histories Publishing, 1991), 55-64.
16. 13th WV Field History, Part 1, Appendix A; CSR, RG 94, M508, Rolls 204-210, National Archives; *Weekly Register*, April 4, 1863. SN 84026817, Library of Congress. See also Appendices B-E.

CHAPTER THREE

THE EARTHEN FORT AT HURRICANE BRIDGE

The location of the Union Fort at Hurricane Bridge has been something of a controversy among researchers. Local oral tradition has offered only limited information as to where it was, and published research on the subject is minimal. Contributing to this is the fact that the Hurricane Bridge battlefield is not one location; it is rather comprised of five different areas, each within roughly one quarter to one half mile of one another, and all are in close proximity to where modern U.S. Route 60 intersects with Midland Trail, i.e. State Route 34. At the time of the battle on March 28, 1863, the James River Turnpike followed a path similar to that of modern Route 60, turning northwest along Hurricane Creek and crossing the bridge along modern Harbor Lane. As earlier discussed, the bridge was then located in the same spot as the modern structure spanning the creek and not the bridge over Hurricane Creek now located on modern Route 60. Locals sometimes also refer to Harbor Lane as Chicken Farm road. Also, the route of modern Midland Trail from the city of Hurricane to Route 60 was not the same path as in 1863. At that time Midland Trail ran from Scary Creek near Scott Depot to the area where modern Main

Street in Hurricane is, connecting with the James River Turnpike near Culloden. (See 1829 Map, p. 60)

Various accounts from oral tradition have suggested the Union fort was in a large, open pasture field immediately adjacent to the modern intersection of U.S. Route 60 and Midland Trail, while others have asserted the fort was located in a field along Harbor Lane on the ridge some one hundred yards west above Hurricane Creek and below the western heights. One researcher also thought the fort was located in a "small, narrow valley" just west of Hurricane Creek, immediately adjacent to the bridge. Further, another part of the local oral tradition suggested the fort was located on the western heights above Hurricane Creek, and only this assertion is consistently supported by both soldier accounts and archeological evidence. Note the fort area is now long replaced by modern housing editions, and the latter were collected prior to development.[1]

The Union fort at Hurricane Bridge was unfinished at the time of the battle, according to Captain James Johnson, although his official report did not provide any clues as to why this was the case. One writer supposed the reason was because Hurricane Bridge was a remote outpost, far removed from the larger battlefields of the war, and as a result, the soldiers knew a large-scale attack on the post was unlikely and lacked a sense of urgency. While it is true that the soldiers in Companies A, B, D and H of the 13th West Virginia garrisoning Hurricane Bridge were used to dealing with occasional raids from Confederate guerillas or cavalry at that point in the war, there is evidence they were in fact in a hurry to complete the earthen fort as quickly as possible.

According to twenty-six-year-old Corporal John Hess, Company D, 13th West Virginia Infantry, the regiment was in quite a hurry to finish the fort, as there were rumors of a strong Confederate presence nearby. Hess was from Meigs County, Ohio, and enlisted at Point Pleasant on August 18, 1862. He wrote to his wife from Hurricane Bridge on February 18, 1863 and provides details of where the Union fort was located: "We are on top of a hill. We can see two miles. We are [building] bilden Breast [works] wirk as fast as we can. Tha say that thar is eight hunderd rebls in 16 miles of us But I think they won't come to us…" Hess was promoted to Sergeant in February 1865 and survived the war without wounding or serious illness. Despite this, progress was slow finishing the earthen fort, probably due to the large number of men in the four companies who were in the hospital or among the "walking ill." Exhausted, sick soldiers are not likely to efficiently dig large amounts of dirt for several hours each day.

Other soldiers commented on the fort's location, including Private Martin Van Buren Edens of Company A, who fought at Hurricane Bridge. He described the fort as located "Between a high hill and circuitous ridge…" Captain Johnson also stated the following: "…the enemy appeared in force and poured a furious fire upon us simultaneously on three sides, from as many different hills, owing to the high elevation of which, and the unfinished condition of our works, exposed our men to a galling cross fire… The enemy's sharpshooters posted on the adjacent heights and armed with globe sighted Rifles were constantly endeavoring to pick off officers and men…" Private Martin Van Buren Edens of Company A further recalled seeing "…Rebs on neighboring ridge... his men on top of each hill," and stated there were Confederates posted "to the left and to the right" of the Union position inside of the earth works, each of which are possible given the following data derived from modern topographical maps.[2]

According to a modern topographical map (p. 57), the highest point on the western heights referred to herein is located on modern Kelly's Drive in Hurricane. The peak is roughly seven- hundred-twenty-feet above sea level, with a flat plateau spanning roughly fifty yards square just below it, having an elevation of six-hundred-eighty-feet. As noted earlier, the western heights are now a residential area, creating a somewhat misleading appearance of being the tallest in the immediate vicinity. (p. 58-59) However, inspection of map data reveals that the eastern heights running parallel to Midland Trail adjacent to the western heights have an elevation of eight to nine hundred feet, and the southern heights parallel to modern U.S. Route 60 adjacent to the western heights are also eight to nine hundred feet above sea level.

In addition, the southern ridge where the Tavern – Stage stop building was located (near the large, modern Red Barn on U.S. Route 60) has elevation of six hundred forty feet, and in 1863 was connected to the base of the southern heights crossing where modern U.S. Route 60 runs. There was a long, sloping elevation in this area that was graded for road construction in the 1950s, which was roughly seven hundred to seven hundred eighty feet above sea level. These factors are important to understanding how the Confederate forces under General Jenkins were able to fire downward into the Union fort and maintain the "galling crossfire" reported by Captain Johnson. There is further evidence indicating that the Confederate sharpshooters (using Whitworth Rifles with Globe sights) were posted on both the eastern and southern heights above the fort, while the main body of Jenkins' troops, likely numbering between two and three hundred, were in line of battle spanning from the ridgeline located by the Tavern house (there is now a large red barn on private land in that area along modern U.S. Route 60) toward the slope running up to the southern heights near modern Lower Coach Road. (See 1829 map p. 60)

Summarily, placing the fort in the "small, narrow valley" on the western bank of Hurricane Creek, as one writer suggested, would have meant imminent disaster for the Union troops for several reasons. First, that area is immediately adjacent to the creek and prone to flooding. Next, it is roughly four hundred feet elevation and less than fifty yards from the ridge where the Tavern was located. This would have allowed heavily concentrated fire from Confederates posted along the latter ridge, causing significant casualties in an unfinished condition, and there were only a small number of Union casualties.[3]

Also, Captain Johnson was doubtlessly aware that if Confederates gained access to the ridge immediately above that spot and to the west, his troops would be completely surrounded and face a murderous fire from the rear also. Placing the fort on the western heights allowed Union troops to command the valley, with excellent visibility from that position; Corporal John Hess noted they could see for "two miles" from there. There is no archeological evidence that the Union fort was located in the open field immediately adjacent to the intersection of Midland Trail and U.S. Route 60, or that it was in the fields located along Midland Trail further north of the intersection. Therefore, with evidence from soldier accounts and artifacts recovered from the fort area, as well as topographical map data, there can be little question the Union fort was located on the western heights, most likely on the plateau just below the peak.[4]

While there is no evidence known to date of precisely how the Union fort at Hurricane Bridge appeared in March 1863, the U.S.

THE EARTHEN FORT AT HURRICANE BRIDGE

Army engineering manuals of the 1860s prescribed a variety of earthen defenses, the most common being a round or octagonal shaped structure, usually with shelters known as "bomb-proofs" dug deep under the walls. The earthen walls were usually eight to twelve feet wide and stood roughly five feet tall. The example below is a common period earthen fort with obstructions known as Abatis, dug in pits surrounding the fort.

Corporal Martin Van Buren Edens of Company A further described the fort with "obstacles" in front and on the sides; these were likely large pits with sharpened sticks known as "Abatis." Edens opined the Confederates "could not surmount" the obstacles. Note there is no evidence that Jenkins' troopers advanced in force along the James River Turnpike toward the fort from the area where it intersected with Midland Trail. The reader is again cautioned there is no evidence known to date that the fort at Hurricane Bridge was made in this fashion; in other words, the sketch and following photographs herein are included only as examples of common earth forts of the Civil War period.[5]

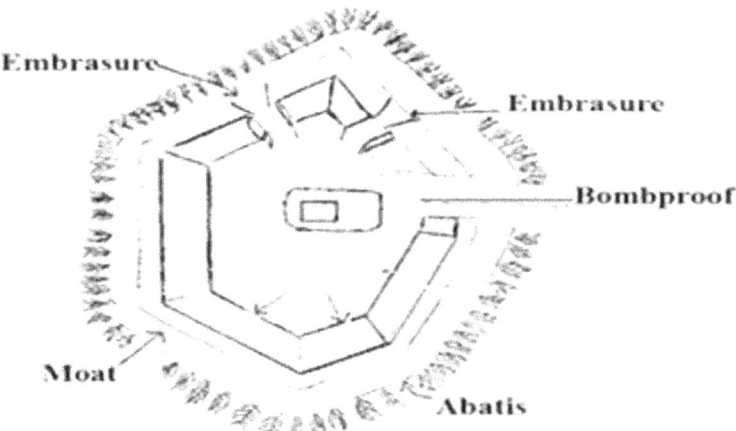

Sketch of typical earthen forts in the Civil War era. Courtesy of U.S. National Park Service. It is unknown whether the earthen fort at Hurricane Bridge had a bomb-proof. This was an interior shelter dug several feet beneath the surface and reinforced by a heavy log and earth covering.

THE BATTLE OF HURRICANE BRIDGE, MARCH 28, 1863

Reproduction of Civil War era earthen fort with Abatis at Petersburg National Battlefield Park. Note this is only an example and may or may not represent the fort located at Hurricane Bridge, as the actual pattern for that structure remains unknown at the time of this writing. The letters of Dr. Samuel G. Shaw, 13th West Virginia Infantry Surgeon, indicate there were several large logs used to reinforce the walls of the earthen fort at Hurricane Bridge.

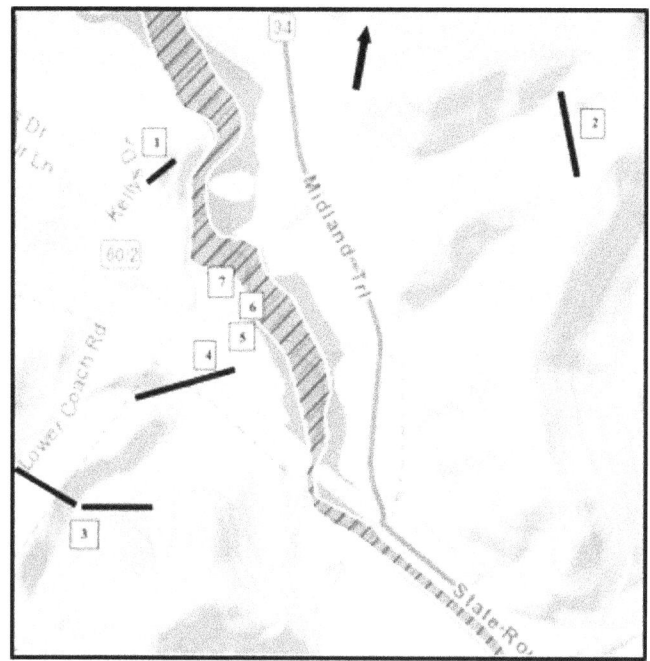

Modern Hurricane Bridge: shows Flood zones along Big Hurricane Creek. WV Maps.com.

1. Union Fort, camp and hospital area: Elevation 680-720 feet
2. Eastern Confederate Sharpshooter Position: Elevation 800-900 feet
3. Southern Confederate Sharpshooter Positions: Elevation 800-900 feet; extends west from Lower Coach Road
4. Confederate Position: Elevation 640-720 feet
5. Tavern – Stage stop
6. Bridge
7. Narrow valley on western creek bank

Note: Harbor Lane (Chicken Farm Rd.) is marked "60/2" and is the route of the James River & Kanawha Turnpike in 1863. Not to be confused with US Route 60, which intersects with Midland Trail and Lower Coach Road. Arrow points North.

View from Union Camp area toward peak of western heights where the Union fort and hospital were located. Photo by Steve Cunningham.

View of Western Heights near modern Kelly Drive with houses removed via Photoshop. This gives an idea of how the area may have appeared in 1863. Photoshop by John F. Kennedy. Photo by Steve Cunningham.

THE BATTLE OF HURRICANE BRIDGE, MARCH 28, 1863

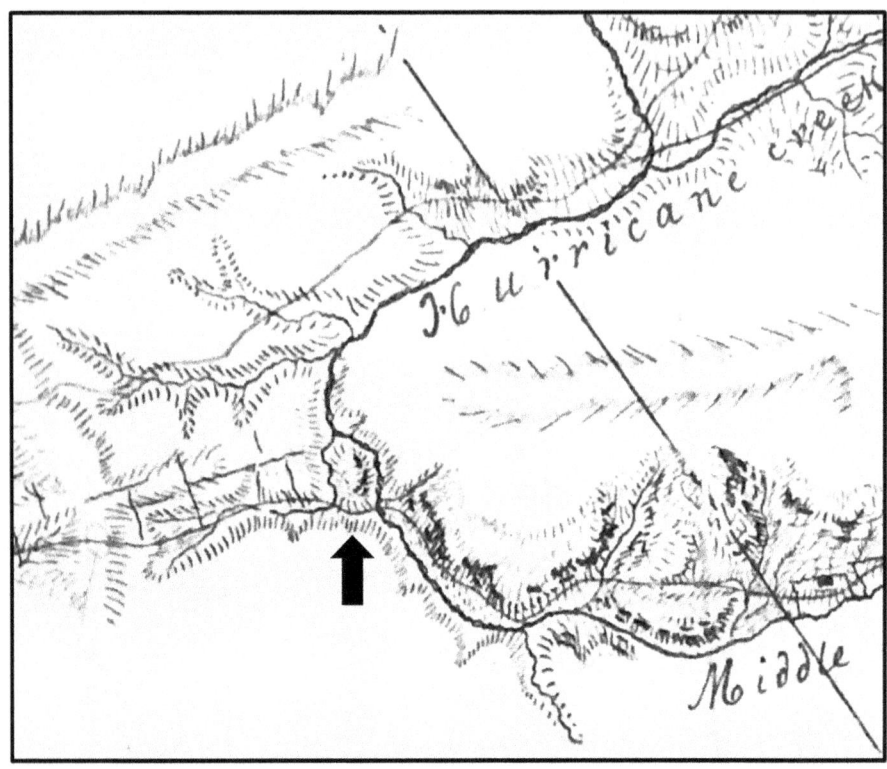

1829 Map Showing Extension of Kanawha Turnpike to the Mouth of the Big Sandy River. C. Crozet, Principal Engineer. Board of Public Works of Virginia, MS-754.3, R6, Part 2. Library of Virginia. Used with permission. View of Hurricane Bridge area showing the James River and Kanawha Turnpike route above the superimposed arrow; the latter also points northwest toward the western heights consistent with modern Harbor Lane.

THE EARTHEN FORT AT HURRICANE BRIDGE

Larger view of 1829 Map Showing Extension of Kanawha Turnpike to the Mouth of the Big Sandy River. C. Crozet, Principal Engineer. Board of Public Works of Virginia, MS-754.3, R6, Part 2. Library of Virginia. Used with permission.

Chapter Three References

1. Dickinson, Jack. *16th Virginia Cavalry.* 1989. (Lynchburg, VA: H.E. Howard, 1989), 17-18. (Hereafter Dickinson, *16th Virginia Cavalry*); Thompson, Robert M. *Fear No Man: The Life of Colonel Milton Jameson Ferguson.* (Genoa, West Virginia: Lulu Press, 2011), 72-73. *(Hereafter Thompson, Life of Colonel Milton Ferguson);* Nelson, Robert H. and Emma L. *Colonel James M. Corns.* (North Charleston, SC: Createspace.com, 2012), 70-74; *Hurricane Centennial,* 4-7; Miller, O.R. Skirmish at Hurricane Bridge; Personal Communications with author: Nathan Lucas, March 20, 2019; Irvin Scarberry March 10, 2019; Sandy Miller Larch, March 25, 2019.

2. 13th West Virginia Field History, Part 1, Appendix A; OR, Series 1, Vol. 19, p. 1083; Civil War Letters of Sergeant John H. Hess, Letter to his wife Samantha Hess, February 18, 1863. Author's Personal Collection (Hereafter J.H. Hess Letters); CSR, 13th West Virginia Infantry, RG 94, M508, Roll 206, National Archives; Edens, Battle of Hurricane Bridge!

3. Personal Communications with author: Nathan Lucas, March 20, 2019; Irvin Scarberry March 10, 2019; Sandy Miller Larch, March 25, 2019; Personal Communication with Terry Lowry, October 18, 2018; Personal Communication with Sandra Duke, March 2, 2019. Also see photos of Whitworth Rifle bullet recovered near fort area on p. 147.

4. *Hurricane Centennial,* 4-7; Miller, O.R. Skirmish at Hurricane Bridge; Weiss, et al. Archeological Survey, 39-42; 51- 59; 63-65; 73-77; Personal Communications with author: Nathan Lucas, March 20, 2019; Irvin Scarberry March 10, 2019; Sandy Miller Larch, March 25, 2019; Personal Communication with Terry Lowry, October 18, 2018; Personal Communication with Sandra Duke, March 2, 2019.

5. Edens, Battle at Hurricane Bridge!; 13th West Virginia Field History, Part 1, Appendix A; OR, Series 1, Vol. 19, 1083; Hurricane Centennial, 4-7; Miller, O.R. Skirmish at Hurricane Bridge. See also Hess, Earl J. *Field Armies and Fortifications in the Civil War: The Eastern Campaigns,* 1861-1864. (Chapel Hill, North Carolina: University of North Carolina Press, 2006).

CHAPTER FOUR

FIELD HOSPITAL AT HURRICANE BRIDGE

The Union garrison at Hurricane Bridge had a regimental field hospital located along the ridge some one hundred yards west of the Union fort. As no less than eight men were found too sick for duty on February 12, 1863, just two days after the Union soldiers arrived at Hurricane Bridge, Colonel William Brown directed Dr. Samuel Glover Shaw, the 13th West Virginia Infantry Assistant Surgeon, to establish a field hospital there on or about February 13, 1863. A resident of Point Pleasant, Mason County, he volunteered to serve in medical capacity for the Union army in 1861. He treated hundreds of sick and wounded men and helped establish the large Union army hospital at Point Pleasant in 1862.

Dr. Shaw was a widower with four daughters, Mary, Rebecca, Judith and Mattie. Mary, his eldest daughter (b. June 12, 1838), was married to George Washington Cargill and resided in Missouri with their son Samuel Glover Cargill (named after his grandfather) when the war began. Ironically, their home was burned by Confederate guerillas during the fierce border warfare occurring there, and she and her son were staying with her sisters in Dr. Shaw's home at Point Pleasant in early 1863 only to again face conflict in a border territory. Dr. Shaw was not initially stationed at Hurricane Bridge on a full-time basis; he traveled between the garrison sites at Winfield, Hurricane Bridge, Coalsmouth, and Mud Bridge treating patients until after the March 28, 1863 battle at Hurricane Bridge, when the combat wounded required his immediate attention, and he was ordered to remain there until further notice.

Shaw left his daughter Rebecca in charge of his affairs at Point Pleasant during his absence and wrote at least six letters to his daughters from Hurricane Bridge during this period. After the war, Dr. Shaw was a prominent citizen of Mason County, West Virginia, and served as chairman of the Battle of Point Pleasant Centennial Committee in 1874 and was instrumental in raising the large monument to Revolutionary War soldiers which still stands in the city. Shaw was also friends with Dr. Andrew Barbee, a physician from Buffalo in Putnam County who raised a company of Confederate infantry known as the Border Rifles.[1]

During his service at Hurricane Bridge, Dr. Shaw accompanied the 13th West Virginia soldiers on several patrol and scouting missions into the Teays Valley area; he observed that area of Putnam County had also suffered from the war, writing to his daughters,"Teays Valley upon one edge of which is the place that I write from is a very beautiful valley. The land lies very finely just undulating enough for drainage. The soil is finely adapted to crops and grains and is well improved. It shows too plainly the effects of this miserable rebellion. Near where I write stand the chimneys and foundations of several buildings that have been burned during the progress of this war."[2]

Dr. Shaw evaluated patients in the field hospital, and if he deemed a patient too ill to remain in that environment, transferred them to the larger army hospitals at Point Pleasant or Gallipolis. One of the few outposts with its own field medical service in the region, the presence of a field hospital at Hurricane Bridge is further evidence there were significantly more troops present than the one hundred fifty reported by Captain James W. Johnson. Some historians, as well as local oral tradition, have suggested that the field hospital and Union encampment were located on the crest of the highest ridge above the small valley parallel to Hurricane Creek at Hurricane Bridge. The James River Turnpike also ran westward from the bridge, about seventy-five yards below the heights where the earthen fort was located, passing along the southern ridge below the heights. Most of that area is now developed into residential areas; however, there are two trails running from the heights down to the field below and to Hurricane Creek that are thought to have been used for accessing water from the camp. During the Civil War, it was common practice to establish garrison camps or outposts on top of hills to avoid water drainage, and also to place them near water sources such as a creek or small river.

In addition to Dr. Shaw, the hospital was also staffed by forty-one-year-old Private Perry Gatewood, who was both Ward Master and Hospital Steward, and forty-three-year-old Private Benjamin Geary of Company D, who was the hospital nurse, appointed in February 1863. Perry enlisted in Company A as a private on August 14, 1862. He was promoted to sergeant, and appointed Hospital Steward in September 1862. However, for unknown reasons, Gatewood was reduced to the rank of Corporal and appointed Ward Master, and continued to serve in that role until July 1864, when he became ill himself with chronic diarrhea. He was reduced to the ranks as private due to disability in September 1864 and was hospitalized at Parkersburg until war's end.[3]

It is a truism that during the American Civil War being under a doctor's care was often more dangerous than not, given period mortality rates. At least one study recently estimated there were around seven to ten deaths from disease for every combat casualty, even with access to medical care. Note the researchers responsible for those data also conceded the latter may be a relative underestimate of the actual number of deaths from disease, likely due to lack of records in small camp hospitals, etc. During the Civil War, diseases played a much stronger role in troop mortality rates than combat, particularly at Hurricane Bridge. Many of the men who volunteered in October 1862 had never been away from their small farms, and when suddenly encamped around several hundred other men, had to adapt to their varying degrees of health and hygiene habits, and many became ill. Unfortunately, with the science of immunology and disease vaccination in their infancy, soldiers' bodies were largely unprepared for the caustic conditions, and they were vulnerable to diseases such as typhoid and pneumonia, two of most deadly camp illnesses in the Civil War.[4]

It is often difficult to ascertain the exact number of troops affected by illness in a given regiment or company due to incomplete data, i.e. incomplete or missing muster rolls, hospital records, etc.

Dr. Shaw left in such haste to arrive at Hurricane Bridge on March 29, that he left his record books in his office at Point Pleasant and had not yet completed his monthly report. Shaw often groused that he found the outpost so remote and isolated that he was having difficulty even getting his mail but noted "One of the retest [worst] privations I suffer here is the daily paper. I have not seen a paper since I have been here and I do not know when I shall."

Yet because this was the first time Shaw had seen the aftermath of any real battles, he also took souvenirs from the wounded soldiers to send home, writing "I send by a boy, Billy Gross, a Confederate belt and some of the balls (bullets) which I have picked up on the battle field. He has promised to call and give it to you. The belt, I forgot to say, I got from one of Jenkins' wounded men." As evidence of the haste in which he had left Point Pleasant on March 29, 1863, Shaw also indicated "I have not changed clothes since I left home" and asked to have clean socks and "drawers" sent when he wrote to his daughters on April 2, 1863.[5]

The 13th West Virginia, however, kept fairly detailed records. Muster rolls, morning reports and other documents from Companies A, B, D and H identify a significant number of soldiers reported as sick in camp or hospital, or at home convalescing from February 8, 1863 through March 28, 1863. Many men were already quite ill when they arrived from Winfield on February 8, 1863, as eight men from Company A were immediately hospitalized shortly after their arrival at Hurricane Bridge. Prior to being ordered to Hurricane Bridge, another twenty-seven men from Companies A, B, D and H were hospitalized at Point Pleasant or sent home due to illness, and remained there through March 28, 1863, so they did not fight in the battle. Four died in the hospital there prior to February 10, and another man died at home.

One man who was sent home was later listed as a deserter, i.e. he never returned. In addition, one private was given a medical discharge due to disability, from the hospital at Point Pleasant prior to February 10, 1863. Many of the sick remained at Hurricane Bridge, such as twenty-one-year-old Corporal Patrick K. Caldwell of Company B, who was deemed too ill to transport to the army hospital at Point Pleasant and died in the field hospital from pneumonia on March 18. Caldwell was from Mason County, and he was present for duty according to a February 28, 1863 muster roll. Morning reports also showed that an average of ten to thirteen men reported to sick call each morning during February and March while stationed at Hurricane Bridge.

Most were not hospitalized and appear to have returned to duty, testifying to the advantages of having access to immediate medical care, despite technological limitations during the nineteenth century. The longer the four companies remained at Hurricane Bridge, the more ill many became. By the morning of March 28, 1863, twenty-nine men were reported as sick in camp and still fought in the battle that day. However, from the time Companies A, B, D and H arrived at Hurricane Bridge on February 8, 1863 until March 28, 1863, seventy-four men were hospitalized or sent home to convalesce. Of that group, more than half were diagnosed with typhoid fever, pneumonia, and some were dually diagnosed with both.

Some other soldiers deserted but returned prior to March 28, 1863, including thirty-four-year-old Private Nathan Burchfield and twenty-two-year-old Harry Sherman of Company D. Twenty-four-year-old Private Fisher Barnette of Company B was found AWOL on February 24, 1863, after receiving word the previous day that his brother was dangerously ill at home. Barnette walked some fifty miles to Mason County, spent a few days with his brother and returned to the company on March 17, 1863. In lieu of Court Martial, Colonel William Brown ordered him on extra duty chopping firewood for the detachment.

It is no surprise that so many men were unfit for duty due to illness on March 28, 1863; between the months of January and March 28, 1863, there were twenty cases of typhoid confirmed in Companies A, B, D and H. Records showed numerous others with unspecified illnesses such as "fever" or simply reflected "sick," although there were also at least twenty-eight with pneumonia. Several men, including twenty-eight-year-old Private Nelson O. Rice of Company B, caught both typhoid and pneumonia and died in the hospital at Point Pleasant. While twenty cases of typhoid is insufficient to call it an epidemic on a larger scale, it certainly was in the Union camp at Hurricane Bridge.[6]

During the 1800s, doctors thought typhoid to be the "prevailing disease" of the period. Patients with typhoid developed rose colored spots on their skin and suffered diarrhea or constipation, fatigue, respiratory distress, fever, and general malaise. While physicians in that era lacked effective treatment for typhoid, they generally understood that survivors could acquire immunity from future exposure, but most did not understand that an otherwise seemingly healthy person could communicate the disease, further spreading the deadly illness to others. The usual treatments were to administer doses of turpentine, brandy, quinine and quinine sulphate, although a handful of military physicians recognized the importance of hygiene and "sanitary measures" to prevent the spread of the disease and isolated the patients from the other troops.

In the years prior to the Civil War, popular lore held that typhoid was caused by "impure air." In 1871, an English physician, William Budd, discovered that typhoid was spread via contaminated water; however, his views did not gain favor with the larger medical community until later. One physician during the Civil War found that it was communicable through human excrement of infected persons in army camps. Hence, army physicians began to take closer looks at how the camps and latrines, or "sinks," were laid out and began to direct commanders to separate the two facilities.

As noted, several men had typhoid or other illnesses while at Hurricane Bridge, but still managed to fight in the March 28, 1863, battle. In Company A, Private Michael Baxter, who was aged twenty-three years, was later sent home to Charleston, where he died in August 1863. Twenty-two-year-old Private Francis A. Cobb, of Kanawha County, was also identified with typhoid and fought on March 28, 1863. He became quite weak afterward and was sent to the regimental hospital at Point Pleasant in May. He survived, although he was killed in action at the Battle of Cedar Creek, October 19, 1864. Private George W. Fitzwater became severely ill in early March as well and also fought on March 28, 1863.

He died in the hospital at Hurricane Bridge on April 20, 1863, from typhoid. Private William M. Crook of Company H was a resident of Wayne County. Aged 18 years, he stood five feet, nine inches, with light hair, dark eyes and a light complexion, and he was employed as a farmer prior to the war. He enlisted August 9, 1862, and fought in the battle, despite having symptoms of typhoid. He was admitted to the field hospital on April 10, 1863, although he soon recovered, as he was discharged from the hospital on or before April 30, 1863. Private Samuel Gordon, also of Company H, became ill from typhoid and was in the hospital there on April 22, 1863, but worsened and was transferred to the hospital at Point Pleasant and then to Gallipolis, Ohio, where he remained until his death on March 15, 1865.[8]

THE BATTLE OF HURRICANE BRIDGE, MARCH 28, 1863

Dr. G.S. Shaw, Regimental Surgeon

13th West Virginia Volunteer Infantry Assistant Regimental Surgeon.
Courtesy City of Hurricane Centennial Commission. Note: The Photo incorrectly
identifies Dr. Shaw as "G.S. Shaw" and should rather state Dr. S.G. Shaw.

Chapter Four References

1. *Hurricane Centennial*, 4-7; Miller, O.R. Skirmish at Hurricane Bridge; Personal Communications with author: Nathan Lucas, March 20, 2019; Irvin Scarberry March 10, 2019; Sandy Miller Larch, March 25, 2019; Personal communication by author with Terry Lowry, author-historian, October 2018; Letters of Dr. Samuel Glover Shaw; Assistant Surgeon, 13th West Virginia Infantry, 1862-1865. Transcript copy from originals held in private collection of Cookie Ambler, March 31, 1863; April 1, 1863; April 2, 1863; April 6, 7 & 8, 1863; and May 6, 1863; Courtesy Betsy Allen and Ron Allen, *Hurricane Breeze*. Shaw's letters were found in a chest following the death of a member of the Cargill family (descendants of Dr. Shaw) and given to the Hurricane Breeze Newspapers in 1966. The letters were transcribed by Irene "Cookie" Ambler and Ron Allen of the Breeze staff to transcribe the text (Hereafter Dr. Shaw Letters).

2. Shaw Letters, April 4, 1863.

3. CSR, 13th West Virginia, RG 94, M507-508, Rolls No. 204-208; WV AG Papers, 13th West Virginia, AR 382, Boxes 20 & 23, Muster Rolls January 1, 1863, to April 10, 1863. WV State Archives.

4. Reilly, Robert F., M.D. Medical and Surgical Care during the American Civil War 1861-1865. *Baylor University Medical Center Journal*, 29(2), 138-142.

5. Shaw Letters, March 31 and April 1, 2, & 5, 1863.

6. Records of the Adjutant General's Office (Record Group 94), Book Records of Union Organizations, 13th West Virginia Infantry, Vol. 4 of 4, Morning Reports, Companies A-D, F-K, March-February 1863. Accession No. E112-115, PI-17. National Archives, Washington DC; CSR, 13th West Virginia, RG 94, M507-508, Rolls 204; 205 & 206; WV AG Papers, Union Regiments, 13th West Virginia, AR 382, Box 23, Company A, B, D and H Muster Rolls, January 1, 1863, to April 10, 1863. WV State Archives.

7. Smith, Dale C. "The Rise and Fall of Typhomalarial Fever: Origins." *Journal of the History of Medicine and Allied Sciences.* (1982), Vol. 37, 182-220; Harris, Dr. Elisha. "Hints for the Control and Prevention of Infectious Disease in Camps, Transports and Hospitals." (New York: United States Sanitary Commission Pamphlet, 1863). Original copy in private collection; Robinson, Nicholas. "Understanding Typhoid in the American Civil War: A Study of Typhoid within the Union and Confederate Armies, 1861-1865." December 2016. Unpublished manuscript completed as an academic research seminar project. University of Wisconsin, 3-8.

8. CSR, 13th West Virginia, RG 94, M507-508, Rolls 204; 205 & 206; WV AG Papers, Union Regiments, 13th West Virginia, AR 382, Box 23, Company A, B, D and H Muster Rolls, January 1, 1863, to April 10, 1863. WV State Archives.

Chapter Five

Confederates in the Hills

During the winter of 1862-1863, Confederate Major General Samuel Jones commanded Confederate troops in western Virginia. Jones' force was camped near Dublin, Virginia, approximately two hundred miles south of Hurricane Bridge. Jones was planning a series of raids in western Virginia that spring, intending to obtain much needed supplies and subsistence. The raids were also meant to create panic among Union citizens, and ultimately turn them away from supporting the war. Major General John D. Imboden and Brigadier General Albert Gallatin Jenkins were to conduct those raids, with Imboden moving across the northern part of the region, and Jenkins traversing the southern territories toward Point Pleasant in Mason County. Their hopes were to not only capture several large supply depots, but also to disrupt regular Union supply shipments from the Ohio Valley.

Imboden was also coordinating with Brigadier General John Hunt Morgan's cavalry, planning an extensive raid through Ohio, Indiana, Tennessee and Kentucky, and western Virginia as a diversion, and also intended to turn public opinion against the war in Union territories. Jenkins' battalion was stationed in Dublin, Virginia, when directed to begin a raid into the Kanawha Valley. His troopers were dismounted, however, as the brigade left their horses in North Carolina to graze for the winter the previous fall. Brigadier General William E. "Grumble" Jones, who was formerly a career army officer, reviewed the plans for Jenkins' men moving across the mountains into western Virginia without their horses and sarcastically observed, "Jenkins and all his men go on foot, and you know how adverse cavalrymen are generally to doing anything on foot."[1]

On this raid, thirty-three-year-old Brigadier General Albert Gallatin Jenkins commanded a cavalry battalion comprised of the 8th and 16th Virginia Cavalry regiments. A wealthy attorney and planter from Green Bottom, Virginia, he earlier attended Marshall Academy (now Marshall University) at age fifteen years and later graduated from Jefferson College in Canonsburg, Pennsylvania, in 1848. An insatiable student, Jenkins attended Harvard Law School next and graduated in 1850. He inherited his father's sprawling plantation at Green Bottom in 1859. In 1856, Jenkins was elected to serve in the United States Congress from the 11th District and took office on March 4, 1857. On March 3, 1861, he resigned from his seat in Congress, knowing Virginia was about to secede from the Union. Jenkins also served in the Confederate Congress during 1862.

Jenkins then served as a representative in the First Confederate Congress just prior to organizing a cavalry company in 1861. Ironically, this was not Jenkins' first time in conflict at Hurricane Bridge; while running for congress in 1856, he engaged in a spirited day-long, public political debate at the site trying to persuade citizens of Putnam and Cabell Counties to support him in the election against the seated Democratic congressman from the district, whom he blamed for supporting Democratic "slavery agitation" that was rapidly beginning to escalate in the country. It is doubtful Jenkins then considered that the once peaceful farmland he debated upon would soon become a killing ground also.[2]

Jenkins' home was located at Green Bottom and included more than one thousand acres spanning both Cabell and Mason Counties. As a result, he was intimately familiar with the people and culture in the area, and because his main objective was to move large stores of supplies across the rough mountainous terrains by wagon train, he included several wagoners and drivers as part of his hand-selected battalion for this operation. Jenkins also took along several pack horses. His Cavalrymen were Companies C, D, E, G, I and K of the 8th Virginia Cavalry, commanded by Colonel James Corns, and Companies D, E, G and K of Colonel Milton J. Ferguson's 16th Virginia Cavalry.

Milton J. Ferguson was from Wayne County and recruited an independent cavalry company in 1861. He soon acquired five other companies, forming a battalion, and was placed under Brigadier General Albert G. Jenkins. In January 1863, Ferguson's battalion was consolidated with four companies of Captain O. Caldwell's battalion to form the 16th Virginia Cavalry Regiment. Ferguson was only recently elected colonel on February 10, 1863, with date of rank January 15, 1863. He was captured in action at Wayne County on February 15, 1864 and sent to Camp Chase, Ohio. He transferred to Fort Delaware on March 25, 1864, although returned after exchange and was later appointed as District Commander in Wayne-Cabell Counties on December 4, 1864, where he remained until the end of the war.[3]

James Corns was also from Wayne County, and he was an architect prior to the war. He initially raised an independent infantry company known as the Fairview Rifles and was elected captain in May 1861. His company transferred into the 8th Virginia Cavalry as Company E on August 4, 1861. Corns was elected Colonel on December 12, 1862, and commissioned on May 15, 1862, at Harrisonburg, Pennsylvania—his commission was hand-delivered by General Robert E. Lee himself. Corns resigned his commission on February 4, 1865. At age thirty-five years, he was described as having a florid complexion, gray eyes, and dark hair and was five feet, eleven inches tall. He eventually surrendered himself to the Federal army at Charleston, West Virginia, and took the Oath of Allegiance on March 11, 1865.

Colonel Corns also had a cousin, James M. Corns, who served in Company K, 8th Virginia Cavalry. He enlisted on May 11, 1861, although he was not present at Hurricane Bridge. He was given furlough to return home to Wayne County to visit his father but was captured on March 3, 1863, and sent to prison at Cincinnati, Ohio. His father, also named James M. Corns, migrated to the United States from England in 1837 and was a Mexican War veteran. He took up residence in Wayne County, Virginia, and during the Civil War, he also occasionally wrote letters to his hometown newspaper describing events of the war. He wrote of his son's capture in the Pontypool Free Press on May 25, 1863, which was published on July 4, 1863:

> "...we have been almost daily subject to fears and disaster from this terrible war. We are in a very bad position here, being on the borders between Virginia and Ohio. The northern army claim this part as within their lines and are most part of the time in possession; but a southern force comes down every two or three months, when the Yankees skedaddle across the Ohio, and return when the enemy has withdrawn. We have had a few battles fought near here, but the number engaged was some few hundreds. The northern soldiers often come to our house, and sometimes search for arms. My son James has been a soldier in the southern army since the commencement of the war. He is in Corn's Regiment, the 8th Virginia Cavalry, noted for its bravery and dashing exploits during the war in Western Virginia. My son came home to see us last March. He came a few days before his regiment came down, and some of my neighbors went out to Pierpont Camp [where the Union troops were then located] to let the Yankees know he was here, and they sent out a part of soldiers to take him. They surrounded the house before we perceived them. I opened the door and turned back to let James know they were there, when I came near being shot for so doing. I received a note from him last week: He was then a prisoner in Cincinnati. I expect he will soon be exchanged. He would have been raised to the rank of Lieutenant in a few days had he not been taken prisoner. His cousin, J.M. Corns, has been colonel of the 8th Virginian Cavalry for the last year, and I am informed he has gone to Richmond with his regiment, and that he will come back a Brigadier General...Yankee soldiers came and took away my horse and saddle. It was the only horse I had, so I am in great difficulty in getting on with my work. I had one horse stolen before. I have managed to put out a small crop of corn, so I think we shall be able to go on for the next winter without much difficulty if left alone by the thievish Yankees. There are but few horses left for farming purposes in this part of the country, for

the Yankees take them from the Secessionists, and the Southern men take them from the Union party. Surely, if the war continues much longer, it will be a very difficult matter to live in this country. Four of my brother William's sons enlisted in the northern army soon after commencement of the war, and his son...was killed when out on a scouting party."[4]

One of the other officers under Jenkins, Major James Nounnan, was involved in numerous smaller raids and skirmishes across the Kanawha Valley earlier in the war, and he was notorious for harassing Union families in the Coalsmouth area, in particular that of Captain John Valley Young, who commanded Company G. Young's home was located near the eastern base of Coal Mountain in Putnam County. His wife, two daughters and two younger sons frequently faced the ire of Confederate military and guerilla forces in the area throughout the war. Often, they came to Young's home at night looking for him; Nounnan brought a small squad of guerillas on September 13, 1862, one day after the massive Federal retreat from the Kanawha Valley. Jenkins' troops on this raid were chosen due to the companies being largely comprised of men from Cabell, Putnam, Wayne and Mason Counties, who were similarly familiar with both the terrain and people inhabiting the areas through which they would pass. In addition, Dr. Charles Timmons, a physician from Buffalo in Putnam County, was the 8th regiment assistant surgeon and was also present on the expedition to care for the wounded and sick.[5]

On February 11, 1863, an unidentified member of the 13th West Virginia Infantry editorialized in the *Wheeling Intelligencer* that it was high time the government allowed Union troops to take stronger action against the guerillas and Confederate troops troubling the Union citizenry, asserting that better results could be had by use of mounted infantry or cavalry against the raiders. The soldier also commented on recently acquired intelligence data that Brigadier General Albert G. Jenkins spent the winter drilling his cavalry brigade as infantry, in anticipation of upcoming spring raids through the region. This would be a significant factor at the small battle occurring at Hurricane Bridge on March 28, 1863, although it appears Federal commanders were unaware of the report. The covert author also reported,

THE BATTLE OF HURRICANE BRIDGE, MARCH 28, 1863

The rebels are still pursuing their old game of arresting and carrying off peaceful, unoffending Union citizens of West Virginia, and in the humble opinion of Union men in this part of the country it is high time that some protection was extended to them - some military organization put on foot that could succeed in making it a little less safe than it is now for mounted rebel guerrillas to venture so far within our lines. About ten days since Benjamin Morris, Sheriff of Putnam county, returning from a sale, was captured ten or fifteen miles in the rear of Putnam Court House, by a portion of Hiram Kirby's mounted guerrillas. On information of which Lieut. Col. [James R.] Hall, commanding a detachment of 13th [West] Virginia, sent out a party with instructions to overtake the rebels, disperse them, and recue Morris, or failing in that to seize a number of the leading secessionists of the neighborhood where the capture was made. The guerrillas could not be overtaken by infantry soldiers, so seven prominent secessionists were brought in by the party and are now held by Col. Hall as hostages for the safe return of Morris. Nothing has since been heard of Morris or his fate. But this is not all. Some two or three days ago, John Winkey, residing near this place, while going up the South side of the Kanawha a short distance to buy furs, was captured by about twenty guerrillas or Herndon's band. His horses were taken and himself stripped of boots and money and forced to "double-quick" for several miles in front of the party, and then set at liberty to find his way home barefooted. The rebels have also captured and carried off, within a short time past, fourteen horses from the lower end of this county, and I am safe in asserting that they will continue to carry off men, horses, and whatever else suits their pleasure so long as we have nothing but infantry to meet them with.

Perhaps the authorities at Wheeling are not aware that the success of the new State is seriously endangered by the very considerable force of rebels now ranging the country between the Kanawha and Sandy rivers. This force will undoubtedly, unless vigorous and effectual measures are taken to prevent it, play an important part in the general election soon to be held...These forces are variously estimated at from eighteen to twenty-five hundred men, and from captured secesh letters, which I have seen, I have no hesitation in saying the estimate is not far from correct. Gen. Jenkins has, agreeably to the best information I can get, about thirty-five hundred dismounted Cavalry in Roanoke county, which he is drilling as Infantry, with the view of using them in the Spring, either as Infantry or Cavalry, or both. Their horses have been sent to North Carolina to be kept through the Winter. All this force, we are told, is to be used to bear upon the vote at the coming election in that part of the new State South of the Little Kanawha river. What is likely to be the result? The prospect certainly is anything but cheering.

And if something cannot be done to prevent the threatened armed interference, and to humble the disloyal inhabitants of the country our success in securing a vote in favor of the new State will be very much jeopardized. Indeed, those who have the best opportunities of knowing and judging, say it will defeat the new State altogether. All of these men have been raised in that portion of the new State referred to; they thoroughly know the people, and every road and by-path within the boundary, and are peculiarly well qualified for the work laid out for them, and success in the accomplishment of their object (the defeat of the new State in the counties below the Little Kanawha) is morally certain, unless the Government can be induced to mount and equip four or five of our Virginia regiments - say the 8th, 9th, 11th and 13th. They also are perfectly well acquainted with the country, the roads and the people, and could and would do more to suppress the abounding manifestations of disloyalty and restore confidence once more to the Union men than twenty thousand infantry. The rebels have been threatening Lieutenant-Colonel [James R.] Hall's command, at Winfield, for some time past, but the Colonel is prepared to render a good account of himself should he be attacked. You may know the danger is real and imminent when Gen. Scammon ordered him to be reinforced without delay. In conclusion I would say, as the game now stands, the chances are that all the detached companies and small commands, stationed all over the country, will be gobbled up in the spring, and we shall have - but on a larger scale - a repetition of the disgraceful scenes that attended Jenkins' raid last fall."[6]

Historically, there has been little agreement among historians as to how many troops Jenkins actually had present on this raid, with estimates usually ranging from 400 to 800 men. Colonel Milton J. Ferguson, commanding the 16th Virginia Cavalry, requested a large supply of infantry weapons and accoutrements from Richmond on March 10, 1863: 160 Richmond Rifled Muskets, 40 Harper's Ferry Rifles, 200 gunslings, 50 waist belts, 224 shoulder straps, 400 haversacks, and 100 cap pouches. Earlier, on March 7, Major General Samuel Jones telegraphed Jenkins, who was at Salem, Virginia, stating, "General: I telegraphed you yesterday that 600 Richmond Rifles had been forwarded to you direct from Richmond. This may enable you to take in your expedition a somewhat greater number of men than we had contemplated. I am trying to procure from Ohio a lot of beef-cattle, to be delivered on this side of the Ohio River, in Mason County; and if the plan succeeds, it is desirable that your force should be large enough to enable you to detail men enough to drive them in this direction, beyond the reach of the enemy. Inform me how many men you can take without unnecessarily encumbering yourself."[7]

On March 8, 1863, Jones telegraphed Major General John Floyd that he proposed to send 500-600 dismounted cavalrymen under Jenkins to the Lower Kanawha. It is noted that Jenkins' battalion was not quite at full strength at this time; many were hospitalized from illnesses at Lewisburg, Virginia, and another forty-fifty were detailed to North Carolina, where the horses were sent for the winter. Captain James W. Johnson, who commanded the Union garrison at Hurricane Bridge, later indicated he learned from captured Confederates that Jenkins had "no less than five hundred men" present. Given these data, a conservative estimate of Jenkins' troop strength is between 500-600 troopers when he arrived at Hurricane Bridge on March 28. Note also that muster roll data for the eleven companies of the 8th and 16th Virginia Cavalry regiments involved at Hurricane Bridge was incomplete. Those rolls lacked consistent demographic data such as age, occupation, etc., allowing descriptive statistical analysis. Appendix F is an example of Jenkins' battalion's muster rolls.[8]

Upon receipt of General Samuel Jones' telegraph of March 7, 1863, directing him to attempt to cross the river into Ohio, Jenkins balked and returned a message stating his doubts about the potential for efficiency and risk of capture driving several herd of beef cattle along with his two battalions. General Jones insisted, however, and telegraphed him again on March 12, 1863,

> General: I received your note of the 9th instant. I regarded the suggestion to drive out beef cattle as offering one additional object which might perhaps be attained by your expedition, especially if you should find it impractable to carry out your plans as discussed and agreed upon. We are greatly in need of beef cattle, and if any private enterprise any cattle are delivered on this side of the Ohio by parties from Ohio, I wish you to give such protection and aid in driving them beyond the reach of the enemy as you can without hazard to the other objects you have in view. If you touch Ohio in your operations, do not permit any wanton destruction of private property. Any private property which you may take, receipt for; the property to be paid for after the ratification of a treaty of peace between the Confederate and United States. If in the course of your expedition you go into Kentucky, it is very desirable that you should do all in your power to conciliate the citizens whom you meet and have intercourse with. Pay as far as you can for all supplies you need and take from them, or give receipts, certified to be paid on presentation to me or the proper officers of the Government in Richmond. If anything happens to oblige you to fall back in haste, which I trust will not be the case, inform me promptly at what point to place subsistence stores for you. You say you expect to strike the Kanawha on the 22d instant. I will instruct Colonel [John] McCausland to move forward and engage the attention of the enemy at Fayetteville on that day. Keep me informed as often as you can of your movements and operations. I pray that your expedition may fulfil your most sanguine anticipations."[9]

Jones' orders to avoid wanton destruction of private property was not fully heeded, however, as would be the case at Hurricane Bridge.

Jenkins was supposed to begin the expedition on March 16, 1863, but he did not leave Dublin until March 18, much to General Jones' annoyance. He telegraphed Jenkins that day worried about the effect a delay would have on Brigadier General John McCausland's brigade, whom he had directed to create a diversion at Fayetteville on the day Jenkins planned to move on the Kanawha Valley. Jenkins marched his dismounted troopers more than two hundred miles on foot in cold, heavy winter weather across the mountains, through Princeton and Raleigh Court House (modern Beckley, West Virginia), and his exhausted men finally reached Howell's Mill in Cabell County on or about March 25, 1863, where they rested a day. They marched from there to Hamlin in Lincoln County on March 27, 1863, and arrived near Hurricane Bridge late that evening, taking position near the intersection of the James River Turnpike and Midland Trail.

Many of Jenkins' troopers were from the immediate areas in Putnam, Wayne and Cabell Counties near Hurricane Bridge, including Private John Patrick Sunderland of Company D, 16th Virginia Cavalry. Sunderland owned a small farm less than five miles from Hurricane Bridge. His family migrated from Ireland, to New York 1856, and settled in Cabell County, Virginia. He enlisted at Mud Bridge in Cabell County on September 6, 1862. Shortly after fighting at Hurricane Bridge, he was captured by Union troops near his home on April 10, 1863. He was confined at Athenaeum prison in Wheeling, West Virginia until April 20, when he was sent to Fort McHenry, Maryland, and then traveled to Fort Monroe in Hampton Roads, Virginia, where he was exchanged and given parole on April 23, 1863. Sunderland returned to his regiment a few days later.

Sunderland was killed in action at Monocacy, Maryland on July 9, 1864, during the initial assault upon the Federal picket line. Serving in Brigadier General John McCausland's Cavalry brigade, the troopers were ordered to dismount, form line of battle and march across an open, but rolling, field. They walked into an ambush; Federal infantry were hiding behind a rail fence in a slight depression of ground and could not be seen until it was too late. The initial volley killed more than thirty men, who were later buried in unmarked trench graves on the battlefield. Sunderland was aged thirty years at the time of his death, and stood 5'11" tall, with a dark complexion, dark hair and gray eyes.[10]

Albert Gallatin Jenkins. Library of Congress.

Colonel Milton J. Ferguson, 8th Virginia Cavalry. Courtesy Wayne County Genealogical Society.

Colonel James Corns, 16th Virginia Cavalry. Courtesy Jack Dickinson.

THE BATTLE OF HURRICANE BRIDGE, MARCH 28, 1863

Brother against Brother

It has become a truism, even cliché, that many soldiers in border states or territories lost their friends, and in some cases, their families over partisan divisions in the Civil War. However, in western Virginia, it was not only commonplace for families to divide, but in many instances, it was more embittered when men joined military units on the opposing sides. Such a case occurred at Hurricane Bridge; one of the lesser known, but more poignant, such stories associated with the war. Corporal John "Jack" Estes of Company D, 8th Virginia Cavalry. At age twenty-five-years, he was the elder of two brothers and the son of Thomas and Mary Estes, two of the earliest settlers in the Hurricane Bridge area. They lived on a small farm along Hurricane Creek and died when Jack was fifteen years old. Jack had worked in Mississippi at age nineteen as a plantation overseer for about two years and returned to Hurricane Creek. When the war broke out in April 1861, the brothers agreed that the youngest, Erasmus, would stay home and tend to the farm while the older two served in the army. In May 1861, Jack enlisted in a local volunteer militia company, the Virginia Guards, and was captured by Union troops and held prisoner in Charleston for about two months. Upon release, he returned home and then enlisted in the 8th Virginia at Hurricane Bridge on September 12, 1862.

Jack's younger sibling, James Monroe Estes, was aged eighteen when the war began. However, he quickly opposed the Confederacy and aligned himself with the local Union men of the area. This enraged Jack, and knowing the danger a Unionist presented to local families, James left their farm to prevent bringing any harm to them. He enlisted in the 3rd Kentucky Infantry, Company E at Camp Robinson, near Louisville on August 17, 1861. He saw heavy action in the western campaigns, and was wounded in the shoulder at the battle of Murfreesboro, Tennessee on January 6, 1863 and returned to duty. James was killed at the battle of Resaca, Georgia on May 17, 1864, and his family had no idea what happened to him. Jack was eventually captured again by Union soldiers in Wayne County, West Virginia in 1864. Specifically, he was arrested by 2nd Lieutenant John Harshbarger of the 3rd West Virginia Cavalry. As a sad epithet to the affair, after the war a family member asked Jack what he would have done if he had to face his brother James on a battlefield during the war, and he is said to have harshly and abruptly responded, "I would have shot him as quickly as I would have shot any other damn Yankee," giving an entirely new perspective to the cliché "brother against brother" in Putnam County.

Another family faced an equally painful division when three members faced each other in combat at Hurricane Bridge. Forty-one-year-old Private William Stewart, Jr. enlisted in Company H, 13th West Virginia at Ceredo, Virginia, on August 12, 1862, and was present in the March 28, 1863 battle. His brother, Henry W. Stewart, is said to have served in Company B, 5th West Virginia Infantry, and another brother, Charles A. Stewart, is supposed to have served in the 14th Kentucky Infantry. However, their youngest siblings, Harrison D. and Thomas H. Stewart, both enlisted in Company K, 8th Virginia Cavalry in October 1861, and were both also engaged at the battle of Hurricane Bridge. William Stewart became ill and was hospitalized at Point Pleasant on May 6, 1864, where he remained until September 1864, when he returned to his unit. Still in failing health, he was again hospitalized at Clarksville Hospital in Maryland in March 1865 and remained until May 17, 1865.[12]

Jenkins' Youngest Trooper

Other than Jenkins himself, perhaps the most infamous of his men was sixteen-year-old Lucien Cincinnatus "Cooney" Ricketts of Guyandotte in Cabell County. He was aged fourteen years in 1861, when he witnessed Albert G. Jenkins making a fiery pro-secession speech in his village. Rickets, whose father died when he was twelve years old, was so impressed he traveled to Jenkins' home located at Green Bottom, near Mason County the next day and enlisted in a company that was forming there known as the Border Rangers. That outfit became Company E, 8th Virginia Cavalry, and was commanded by Captain James Corns of Ceredo.

The spunky, aggressive youth quickly became the regiment's mascot, and Jenkins behaved quite paternally toward the young soldier. Ricketts and his brother had both previously attended Marshall College (now Marshall University) in Cabell County. He excelled in academics and eventually gained admission to the Virginia Military Institute in August 1863. Jenkins accompanied him on the matriculation day and even paid for his tuition, which was $400. Rickets later served with the Corps of Cadets when they were sent to assist in the Battle of New Market, Virginia on May 18, 1864, and he heroically saved an officer who was severely wounded by pulling him out of the line of fire.[13]

Another of Jenkins' men, Sergeant James D. Sedinger, also of Company E, 8th Virginia Cavalry, was born in Monroe County, Virginia in 1838. He originally enlisted in a militia company known as the Border Rangers led by Jenkins at Green Bottom in late 1860. They were sworn into Confederate service on May 29, 1861. Sedinger kept a detailed war time diary record of his experiences, and he was present at Hurricane Bridge that morning on March 28, 1863. He re-enlisted in Company E, 8th Virginia Cavalry on April 30, 1862 at Jenkins' home in Green Bottom and was involved in several raids and skirmishes in the Kanawha Valley, including the Battle of Scary Creek in Putnam County on July 17, 1861.

He was promoted to 3rd Corporal in 1861 and was again promoted to 2nd Sergeant in early 1862. Sedinger recalled the following incident occurring just before the battle, which, although humorous, also provides important details of Jenkins' men's general physical appearance at the time of the battle, after having marched through rough, mountainous terrain in harsh winter weather:

> On the 24th of March 1863, we broke camp for a march to the Ohio River on foot. By the time we reached Cabell County half the boys was barefooted. We reached Hamlin [now Lincoln County] about dark, and put out pickets on all the roads. About daylight the morning of the 28th the sentinel on the road towards Hurricane brought in a man with a two-horse team who had been hauling bacon to the Yanks at Hurricane Bridge. The man thought we were Yanks and told us all he knew. While the officer was talking to him, Rod Noel of the old Company noticed that he had on a good pair of shoes. Rod was barefooted and said to him, "Could or would you give an old Confederate soldier a good pair of shoes?" That was the first intimation that the man had that we were Rebels. He said to Rod that he would if he had

any but those he had on. Rod asked him if he had any more at home. He told him "Yes." "Well," Rod said to him, "Give me them, you can stand it better to ride home barefooted in your wagon than I can do to walk." The man pulled off his shoes and gave them to Rod. He was scared so badly he did not know what he was doing. He and his wagon and horses were sent on to the General who told him to go home and behave himself."

Private Roderick R. Noel was a member of Company G, 8thVirginia Cavalry. He left his job as a farmer and enlisted on September 1, 1861 at Guyandotte, at age eighteen years. Noel stood 5'4" tall, had gray eyes and red hair, with fair complexion. Noel was known as an aggressive, difficulty personality. He was later captured by the 7th West Virginia Cavalry in Wayne County on February 24, 1865, sent to Athenaeum Prison at Wheeling and transferred to Camp Chase, Ohio on February 24, 1865.

He gave the guards so much trouble there that one of the officers described him as a "bad man" on the prison roll. This was not the first time Noel and his friends had relieved a Union man of his shoes; Sedinger elsewhere in his diary wrote that they had "simply robbed a loyal Union man of his shoes," in spite of Jenkins issuing strict orders forbidding his troopers to plunder from civilians while in the Kanawha Valley. It is also important to note this was not the first or last patrol or skirmish they had fought dismounted; Sedinger makes numerous references to fighting dismounted across the war, despite General Samuel Jones' blithe earlier presumption of Jenkins' cavalrymen.[14]

Lucien C. "Cooney" Ricketts, Co. E, 16th Virginia Cavalry.
West Virginia State Archives.

Captain Jonathan Hankins, Co. C, 16th Virginia Cavalry. Private Collection. Used with Permission. Hankins enlisted on May 29, 1861 at Tazewell, Virginia. He survived the war without wounding, capture or hospitalization and took the Oath of Allegiance at Charleston, West Virginia on June 15, 1865. Source: Source: CSR, 8th Virginia Cavalry, RG 94, M324, Roll 147, National Archives.

Sergeant Daniel Clinton Lovett, Co. G, 8th Virginia Cavalry. Private Collection. Used with Permission. Lovett enlisted in 1862 at Wood County at age twenty-one years, and was captured near Logan, West Virginia on December 5, 1864. He was sent to Camp Chase, Ohio for the remainder of the war. This image shows him wearing an officer's uniform thought to be from militia service, although it is not clear to which regiment he belonged. Source: CSR, 8th Virginia Cavalry, RG 94, M324, Roll 84, NationalArchives.

1st Sergeant Calvin Cyfers, Co. E 16th Virginia Cavalry. Private Collection. Used with permission. Cyfers enlisted September 6, 1862 at Wayne County as a private. Appointed 1st Sergeant on September 15, 1862 and was AWOL March 25, 1864. Cyfers was born in Smythe County, Virginia, and was aged forty-eight years at enlistment, and worked as a blacksmith. He was five feet, ten inches tall, with light complexion and dark hair, and blue eyes. He was listed as a deserter at Guyandotte in April 1865. Source: CSR, 16th Virginia Cavalry, M324, Roll 146, National Archives.

Private John A. Miller, Co. G, 8th Virginia Cavalry. Private collection. Used with permission. Miller is aged nineteen years in this 1860 image. He enlisted on May 13, 1861 and survived the war without wounding, capture or hospitalization. He took the Oath of Allegiance at Charleston, West Virginia on May 8, 1865. Miller was five feet, six inches tall with blue eyes and had "many whiskers" at the end of the war. Source: CSR, 8th Virginia Cavalry, RG 94, M324, Roll 84, National Archives.

THE BATTLE OF HURRICANE BRIDGE, MARCH 28, 1863

Private Mark Hale Sesler Co. C, 8th Virginia Cavalry. Private Collection. Used with Permission. Sesler enlisted April 27, 1862 at Crumps, Virginia, and was present until captured at October 19, 1864 at Cedar Creek and sent to Point Lookout, Maryland. He took the Oath of Allegiance on June 19, 1865. Sesler was five feet, five inches tall, with blue eyes and brown hair, and fair complexion. Hale resided at Grayson, Virginia, prior to the war and was a blacksmith. Source: CSR, 8th Virginia Cavalry, RG 94, M324, Roll 85, National Archives.

Private Charles Perrow Co. C, 8th Virginia Cavalry. Private Collection. Used with Permission. Perrow enlisted June 22, 1861 and became severely ill in July and was sent home on sick furlough and return to duty in November 1861. Perrow was later promoted to Corporal, and was captured at Lynchburg, Virginia on June 17, 1864. He was imprisoned at Wheeling, WV. Source: CSR, 8th Virginia Cavalry, RG 94, M324, Roll 84, National Archives.

Chapter Five References

1. Dickinson, Jack. *16th Virginia Cavalry*, 17-18.
2. Dickinson, J. L. *Jenkins of Green Bottom*. (Charleston, WV: Pictorial Histories Publishing, 1988), 30-59.; Heckler, Kenneth. Albert G. Jenkins. *Herald Advertiser*, August 13, 1961.
3. CSR, 8th Virginia Cavalry, RG 94, M324, Roll 146, National Archives.
4. CSR, 16th Virginia Cavalry, RG 94, M324, Roll 82, National Archives; Corns, James M. Letter to Pontypool Free Press, Monmouthshire, England, July 4, 1863. Cited in Nelson, and Nelson, *Colonel James M. Corns*, 71.
5. Civil War Diary of Sarah Francis Young, (a.k.a. "Sallie) 1861-1862; September 12 & 13, 1862, 12-15; In J.V. Young Letters, Roy Bird Cook Collection, Call No. A&M 0895, West Virginia Regional History Collection, West Virginia University Library, Morgantown WV; Miller, Skirmish at Hurricane Bridge; Dickinson, *16th Virginia Cavalry*, 17-19.; Dickinson, Jack L. *8th Virginia Cavalry*. (Lynchburg, Virginia: H.E. Howard, 1986), 111. (Hereafter Dickinson, *8th Virginia Cavalry*)
6. "Another Sheriff Captured." Wheeling Intelligencer, February 21, 1863. Point Pleasant, Va., Written by unidentified 13th WV soldier on February 11, 1863. Library of Congress.
7. Comstock, 131; CSR, 16th Virginia Cavalry, RG 94, M324, Roll 146, National Archives; OR, Series 1, Vol. 25, Part 2, 657-658.
8. OR, Series 1, Vol. Vol. 51, Part 1, 176; CSR, RG 94, M324, Roll 85, National Archives; Miller, O.R. Skirmish at Hurricane Breeze; 13th WV Field History, Part 1, Appendix A. For a good composite of available information from rolls, the reader is referred to Jack Dickinson's books on the 8th and 16th Cavalry regiments; each contain detailed Appendices summarizing available CSR and Muster Roll information on each company.
9. Ibid., 672; Dickinson, *8th Virginia Cavalry*, 28; 37-38.
10. CSR, 16th Virginia Cavalry, RG 94, M324, Roll 149, National Archives; Dickinson, *16th Virginia Cavalry*, 46-49; 115.
11. CSR, 8th Virginia Cavalry, RG 94, M324, roll 82; CSR, 3rd Kentucky Infantry and 3rd West Virginia Cavalry, M397, roll 170 and M508, Roll 25, respectively, National Archives; Upper Vandalia Historical Society *History of Putnam County, West Virginia*. Vol. 2, (Charleston, West Virginia: Pictorial Histories Publishing, 1967), 102-104.

12. Napier, Mose A. *Ceredo: It's Founders & Families*. (Ceredo, West Virginia: The Phoenix Systems, 1989), 9-10; CSR, 13th West Virginia Infantry, RG 94, M 508, Roll 209; 5th West Virginia Infantry, RG 94, M508, roll 130; 14th Kentucky Infantry (US), RG 94, M397, R279; 8th Virginia Cavalry, RG 94, M324, Roll 85, National Archives; Dickinson, Wayne County, 58-59; See also Appendix E, 13th West Virginia, Company H Muster Roll, pp. 189-191. Note that Henry W. Stewart does not appear on muster rolls from the 5th West Virginia Infantry; similarly, Charles A. Stewart does not appear on muster rolls from the 14th Kentucky Infantry. In addition, Harrison D. Stewart does not appear on the 8th Virginia Cavalry muster rolls. Their father, William Stewart, owned the parcel of land where the modern Veteran's Affairs Medical Center is now located in Spring Valley, West Virginia.

13. Dickinson, Jack L. Cooney Ricketts: A Child of the Regiment. (Charleston, WV: Pictorial Histories Publishing, 2001), 17, 51-60; 61-72; CSR, 8th Virginia Cavalry, RG 94, M324, Roll 85, National Archives.

14. Sedinger. J.D. Diary of a Border Ranger. 1889. Typescript of Original manuscript. WV State Archives. (Hereafter Sedinger, Diary); Sedinger, J.D. "War Time Reminiscences of James D. Sedinger, Company E, 8th Virginia Cavalry (Border Rangers)." West Virginia History, (1992), Vol. 51, 55-78. (Hereafter Sedinger Wartime Reminiscences); CSR, 8th Virginia Cavalry, RG 94, M324, roll 84, National Archives.

Chapter Six

BATTLE AT HURRICANE BRIDGE MARCH 28, 1863

A post-war recollection written by Frederick "Fred" Conner refers to the fight on March 28, 1863, as the "Engagement at Hurricane Bridge." Conner states, "In the winter of 1863, a report became current within the Confederate lines that a vast quantity of government stores were deposited at Point Pleasant, Mason County, and that a number of horses were corralled at the same place. Accordingly about the 20th of March a detachment of about 800 men consisting of portions of the 8th and 16th Virginia Cavalry commanded by General Jenkins with Dr. Chas. Timmons of Buffalo as Surgeon began to march from Dublin Depot to Point Pleasant over the mountains two hundred miles distant. On the 28th of the same month the detachment reached Hurricane Bridge in the southern part of Teays Valley…"[1]

Historians have long speculated as to why General Jenkins chose to fight at Hurricane Bridge, as it appears to have been a last-minute decision. He could have easily circled around the post out of sight, and reached Point Pleasant without having to fight, according to some writers. Recalling that his immediate objectives were to distract attention from another raid being conducted by Generals William "Grumble" Jones and John D. Imboden in the northern area of western Virginia; and also to capture the large store of supplies and horses held by the Union garrison at Point Pleasant, as well as to receive the herd of beef-cattle from Confederate sympathizers in Ohio, it is not hard to ascertain why Jenkins chose to attack. Prior to his arrival at the village of Hamlin in what is now Lincoln County, West Virginia, on March 27, 1863, Jenkins supposed the Hurricane Bridge area was unoccupied by Federal troops. However, at Hamlin he was given accurate information by a citizen that there was now a garrison of Union troops occupying Hurricane Bridge.

Hence, when Jenkins approached Hurricane Bridge early in the morning of March 28, 1863, he was acutely aware that he outnumbered the Federals there at least four to one. He also knew that if his raid was to be successful, he would have to return south by the same route, only he would be more encumbered by the heavy wagon train loaded with supplies and a herd of beef cattle, and he would have to fight them anyway. Jenkins was also aware that Federals knew he was in the area, and avoiding a fight would only allow the garrison at Hurricane Bridge to send for reinforcements, making a conflict on his return trip even more arduous. Although it seems prudent that he chose to fight then since he outnumbered the Federals, rather than later under more adverse conditions, at least one writer concluded that Jenkins' decision to attack was "arrogant," noting the ultimate result was nothing more than a "sullen withdrawal."[2]

Weather conditions on March 28, 1863, were cold and damp. According to one soldier, "...we have had a great deal of rain here for the last week..." making the roads muddy and wet; many of the Union soldiers were very ill, and, as noted, many of the Confederates were barefoot and were all nearly exhausted from the two-hundred-mile march. As Jenkins stealthily approached, he aligned his main body of Confederate troops along the James River Turnpike, facing west near where the turnpike intersected with Midland Trail, and ordered them to halt. Observing the unsuspecting Union pickets posted near Hurricane Bridge, Jenkins quietly ordered his sharpshooters, numbering approximately two hundred, to take position on the heights to the south and east, each roughly four tenths to a half mile from the fort. Jenkins then ordered the main body of his force to position along the ridgeline near the Tavern, extending southwest toward the base of the southern heights. He now had the Union fort in a vice-grip, and the Union pickets, or sentries, guarding access to the earthen fort, were completely unaware of the Confederates.[3]

Sergeant J.D. Sedinger described how events began to unfold at Hurricane Bridge on the morning of March 28, 1863:

> We marched all night, nearly the next night, arriving at Hurricane Bridge about daylight. The General sent in a flag of truce demanding surrender. The Captain in command refused and moved into a fort that was nearby and held it against us as we had no artillery with us. John Payne of the Company was killed…

According to one historian, Jenkins sent Major James Nounnan with a flag of truce bearing a message for Colonel Brown, commanding the 13th West Virginia. Brown was not present, but rather it was Captain James Johnson, commanding the garrison, who received the message from his pickets. A soldier in Company A, twenty-three-year-old Corporal Martin Van Buren Edens, indicated that it was "Samuels" who carried the flag of truce, and accompanied Major Nounan. Corporal Edens refers to thirty-three-year-old 1st Lieutenant Alexander H. Samuels of Company D, 8th Virginia Cavalry, under Captain James Corns of Wayne County. Samuels was a merchant prior to the war, and stood 5'9" tall, with black hair, black eyes and dark complexion. He was commissioned on May 14, 1862. Corporal Martin Van Buren Edens was from Mason County, Virginia, and enlisted on August 15, 1862, at Charleston, Virginia. He was promoted to Corporal on September 23, 1862 and was later reduced to private in June 1864 for unstated reasons.

Edens was "slightly" wounded at the battle of Winchester on September 19, 1864 and spent the remainder of the war at the army hospital in Gallipolis, Ohio. Fred Conner, a former slave from Putnam County, traveled with the 36th Virginia Infantry as a servant, and he knew many of the soldiers in Jenkins' command personally. He wrote an account of Hurricane Bridge also, commenting that when Major Nounnan approached the Union pickets, he was taken under flag of

THE BATTLE OF HURRICANE BRIDGE, MARCH 28, 1863

truce (with Lieutenant Samuels) to Captain James Johnson's headquarters, which were located in a field about one hundred yards to the north of the bridge.[4]

Upon receipt of Jenkins' note, Captain Johnson realized that Jenkins expected to find Colonel William Brown inside the fort commanding. He later reported to Colonel Brown what took place that morning:

> April 3, 1863…I have the honor to make the following report of the assault made upon this post. The rebel Genl Jenkins and his command on the 28th inst. about 6 O.C. in the morning on the 28th Inst. our pickets brought in a flag of truce with the following from Jenkins: 'Col, I now have an overwhelming force so disposed as to completely surround you, and cut off your retreat, a humane desire to avert the loss of life, and this is need to demand your surrender, in the event of your compliance, and the surrender in good faith of all forces under your command, they shall receive the treatment warranted by the usages of War, and both officers and men will be paroled. Twenty minutes will be allowed for the consideration of this note and to return reply. I am Colonel, very Respectfully, Yr Obt Servt, AG Jenkins, Brigadier Genl C.S.A.

Captain Milton Stewart, Company B, noted in his next morning that the battle began around 5:45 a.m. Johnson continued, "On receipt of the above note I immediately sent him reply, that I should not surrender the forces under my command, unless forced to do so by an exhibition of his boasted strength. And immediately set about making the best possible disposition of the limited forces under my command. In fifteen minutes we were ready for action. All available force remaining about 150 effectives and were drawn up inside our fortifications when the enemy appeared in force…" Captain Johnson apparently either did not know Jenkins' actual strength, thought he was bluffing, or both. He may also have over-estimated his own firepower given that the condition of the earthen fort was unfinished, but either way, he chose to fight.

Once he declined to surrender, Johnson knew attack was imminent. He hastily ordered his pickets inside the unfinished fort and gave the orders for the four companies to "fall in" and form into an organized rank formation. The fort was yet unfinished primarily due to so many men being down with illness or hospitalized. Some researchers have asserted it was because the inexperienced Union soldiers lacked a sense of urgency, thinking they were too far away from larger theatres of the war to worry about large-scale attacks. However, to the contrary, Corporal John H. Hess of Company D wrote on February 18, 1863, that they were building the earth works "as fast as we can." It is also unlikely their slow progress was due to Captain Johnson lacking adequate intelligence information as to the location of any Confederates in the vicinity. Hess also indicated they were well aware of a large Confederate force lurking in the region, informing his wife the regiment was "in a bad place" and vulnerable to attack. Hence, the incomplete condition of the fort was not due to a lack of awareness or minimizing the potential threat on Captain James Johnson's part.

As the Union soldiers took their places along the roughhewn logs lining the muddy walls of the fort, and silently stood awaiting orders to open fire, Corporal John H. Hess and others quietly thought of their wives, families and friends at home. A few even looked forward to the coming fight, wanting to prove themselves in their first real combat experience. Captain Johnson then ordered twenty-three-year-old Sergeant Hezekiah Scott of Company D, the regimental color bearer, to raise the colors, and Johnson posted the color guard behind the line of battle, which was roughly formed along the parapet of the earthen fort. Near the center where Johnson also stood were also two lieutenants, one of whom was 1st Lieutenant Emory J. Bridgeman, the regimental Adjutant, who, unknowingly, was in his last few moments of life on this earth.[5]

13th West Virginia Infantry, 1862 regimental colors. Made by Horstman Brothers & Co., Philadelphia, PA. Courtesy of West Virginia State Museum. This is the regimental flag carried by Sergeant Hezekiah Scott on March 28, 1863.

Sergeant Scott was appointed Color Sergeant in December, and he carried the colors until promoted to 1st Sergeant on February 7, 1864. Scott was later wounded at the Second Battle of Kernstown, Virginia, on July 24, 1864. Corporal Martin Van Buren Edens of Company A remarked later that the Union soldiers were "cool as ice" as they fell into ranks within the earth works to repel Jenkins' attack. This is an interesting observation, as they were about to face their first fight operating as a cohesive force; many of them had never seen any action and were about to "See the Elephant."

The latter was a Civil War period colloquialism meaning to see combat for the first time. After receiving Captain James Johnson's report, Colonel William Brown later succinctly summarized the events of that morning:

> On the morning of March 28th, a rebel force numbering eleven companies of the 8th and 11th [16th] Regiments of Virginia Rebel Cavalry (dismounted) under the command of General A.G. Jenkins, appeared before that place and demanded the surrender of the force; which was refused by Capt. James Johnson who commanded the post. A battle ensued which lasted from 6 am until 11 o clock am." Brown's estimate of Jenkins' companies was not far off; Jenkins had ten, not eleven, companies present at Hurricane Bridge.[6]

Captain Johnson left a more graphic picture of the Federals' predicament, recalling further that within about twenty minutes of his refusal to surrender, Jenkins' sharpshooters, posted on the three hills above and surrounding them, opened fire in force. Johnson had no idea heretofore that the Confederates were on the surrounding hillsides, much less that they bore deadly globe sighted rifles.

THE BATTLE OF HURRICANE BRIDGE, MARCH 28, 1863

Letter written by Corporal John H. Hess, Co. D, 13th West Virginia Volunteer Infantry, February 18, 1863 shortly after arriving at Hurricane Bridge. Author's Collection.

BATTLE AT HURRICANE BRIDGE MARCH 28, 1863

As five to six hundred bullets zipped through the air around he and his men, Johnson knew it was time to fight. Jenkins' firing positions from the three surrounding heights created a triangular shaped killing zone and resulted in what Johnson described as a "galling crossfire." He also indicated Jenkins' sharpshooters had the advantage of "Globe-sighted Rifles."

This weapon was known as a Whitworth Rifle, a .451 caliber, single-shot muzzle loader made by British Armorer Sir Joseph Whitworth of Manchester, England. Whitworths had a telescopic rear sight adjustable to 1,200 yards, with a "globe" sight located on the muzzle, enabling the user to accurately estimate target distance based on its relative size observed through the globe sight. The Confederate army purchased several hundred Whitworth Rifles from England during the Civil War at a cost of $1,000.00 each. The bullets were octagonally shaped. While the exact number of Whitworth rifles Jenkins had on hand is unknown, it is doubtful there were more than a few due to the cost.

When shipped from the armory, each Whitworth also came with 1,000 rounds of ammunition and had an effective range of 800 to 1,000 yards. They weighed 9.1 pounds loaded, and shooters usually had to rest the rifle against a tree branch for stability to ensure maximum effectiveness. It is noted that several writers have mistakenly identified the Whitworth Rifles used at Hurricane Bridge as "scoped" rifles. While Joseph Whitworth was manufacturing those at the time of this battle, Globed sights were different than a telescopic lens. The latter were typically mounted on the top or side of the barrel and were much easier to operate than the complex sighting procedure required with Globe sights.[7]

As his troopers were dismounted, and having just marched over two hundred miles, Jenkins wisely kept his distance from the Union fort. He established his command position on the bottom ground located between the surrounding heights near the James River Turnpike. Jenkins deployed his troops as follows: On the eastern heights located roughly four tenths of a mile from the Union fort, he placed about one hundred sharpshooters, some of whom were armed with Whitworth Rifles. On the ridgeline to the immediate right of the fort, roughly three tenths of a mile south, he posted nearly four hundred troopers armed with Richmond .69 rifled muskets and 1855 Harper's Ferry Rifles, also .69

caliber. A few researchers have conjectured that Jenkins' Confederates were carrying double-barreled shotguns in 1863; however, according to Private Thomas Copenshaver, Company A, 8th Virginia Cavalry, while many in fact carried double-barreled shotguns from home when they volunteered in 1861, (and also had to furnish their own equipage as well as horses and saddles) by 1863 those had been replaced with arms "supplied by the Federals."

On Jenkins' upper far left, located on the hills some one to two hundred yards south (south of U.S. Route 60) he posted roughly another one hundred sharpshooters, also armed with Richmond .69 caliber rifles, .58 caliber 1855 U.S. rifled muskets, and some with Whitworth .45 rifles. As earlier noted, Jenkins also had access to six hundred Richmond Muskets when he began the expedition; these were rifled using captured ordnance equipment from the former Federal Arsenal at Harpers Ferry in 1861. The 13th West Virginia, on the other hand, was armed with M1842 Rifled Muskets, .69 caliber, which was the standard U.S. Army issue weapon at that time. An exception was Company A, who received a shipment of 1862 Austrian Lorenz Rifles in October 1862, after turning in their old .69 caliber percussion conversion rifled muskets. Knowing he had sharpshooters armed with globe sighted Whitworth rifles was also likely a factor in Jenkins' decision to attack at Hurricane Bridge, as it clearly provided a tactical edge.

Captain Johnson later recalled, "...the enemy appeared in force and opened a furious fire upon us simultaneously on three sides from as many different hills, owing to the high elevation of which and the unfinished condition of our works, exposed our men to a most galling crossfire." Dr. George Shaw, the 13th West Virginia Assistant Surgeon, was thankful that he did not have to treat severe casualties from artillery wounds at Hurricane Bridge. He wrote to his daughter from Point Pleasant a few days later, "At the time of the fight the fort was not completed and would have been no protection from artillery...It certainly is a very difficult place to fortify against artillery, there are high hills all around it in nearly every direction commanding this place."[8]

As the battle opened, firing was rapid and heavy. Soon, a dense smoke soon filled the air and hovered around the fort and adjacent heights, limiting the visual field of both the Union and Confederate soldiers. When Captain Johnson saw Jenkins' men appear "in force" along his right center, i.e. the ridgeline located near the tavern some one to two hundred yards south, he hurriedly barked out orders for Companies D and H, the two center companies, to "fire at will" upon the sharpshooters located on the southern heights to their right.

This command created what Johnson later described as an "animated," intense and persistent line of fire on Confederates in closer proximity to the fort, rather than allowing his men to suffer periods of minutes without being able to fire, waiting on opposite ranks to reload and be given orders to fire again. The typical soldier in that era was expected to fire three aimed shots in one minute, using a single-shot muzzle loading weapon. This required a great deal of poise and concentration to execute, particularly when the officers used sequential firing commands such as "fire by company" or "fire by ranks" and in many instances, "fire by battalion," which was one single shot taken by the entire group of four companies in unison toward the advancing force, intended to inflict maximum casualties.

As the battle pitched, Jenkins' sharpshooters pinned the Federals down inside the earthen fort. Corporal George W. Fulwiller, Company H, could not stand the tension and took "French Leave," i.e. deserted his post, running from the field during the fight. Fulwiller enlisted October 9, 1862 at Point Pleasant. Reported as "Missing in Action", the officers said he had deserted during the battle. Fulwiller was later arrested and confessed, then confined in Charleston. Colonel Brown reduced him to the ranks, but he eventually returned to duty. Fulwiller became ill in July 1864 and was hospitalized until the end of the war.[9]

THE BATTLE OF HURRICANE BRIDGE, MARCH 28, 1863

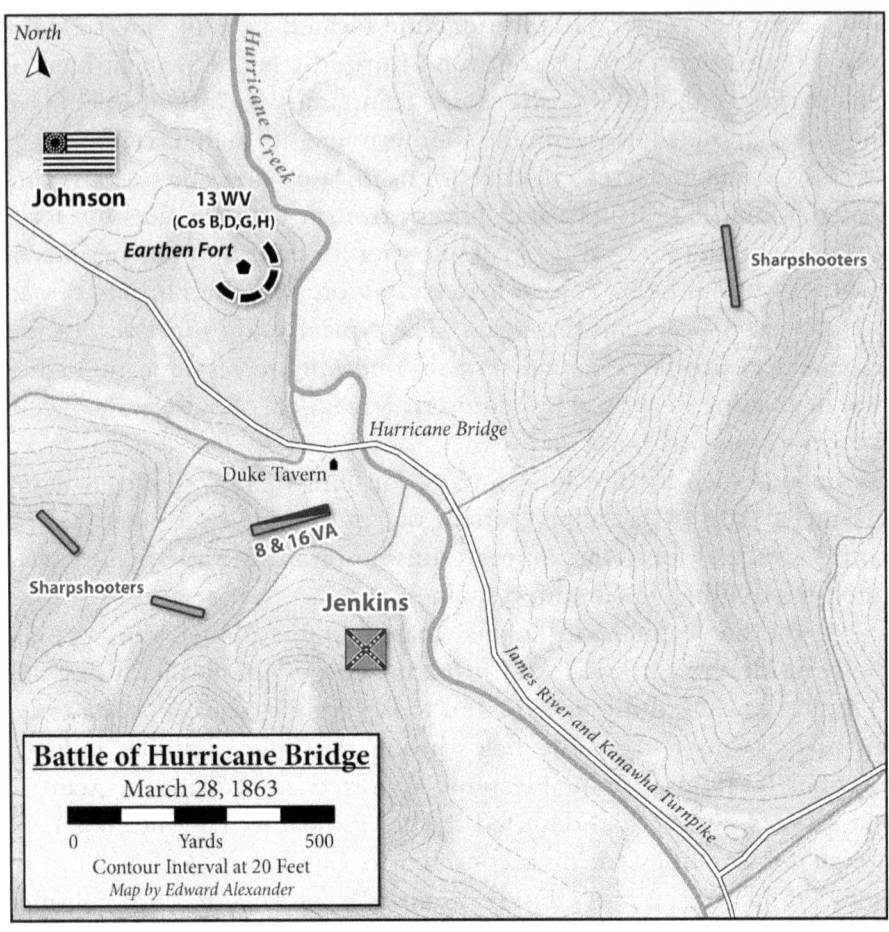

BATTLE AT HURRICANE BRIDGE MARCH 28, 1863

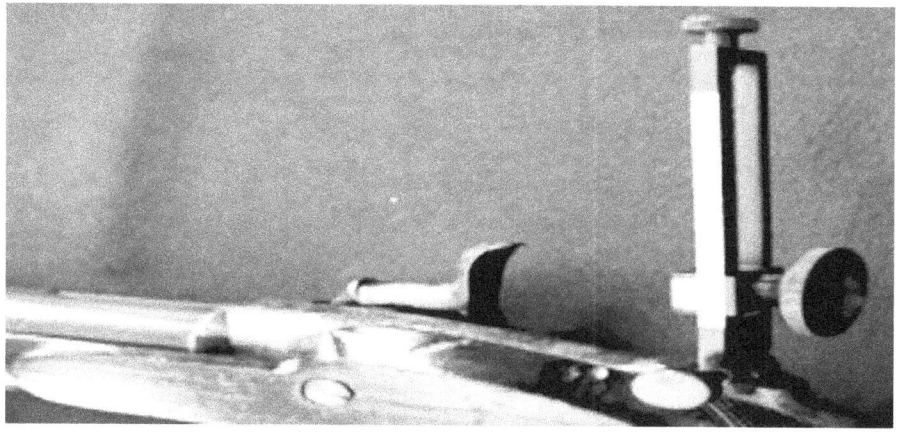

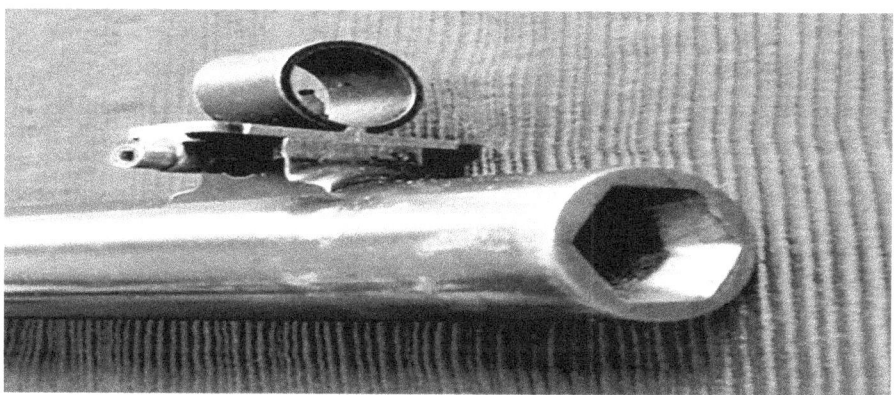

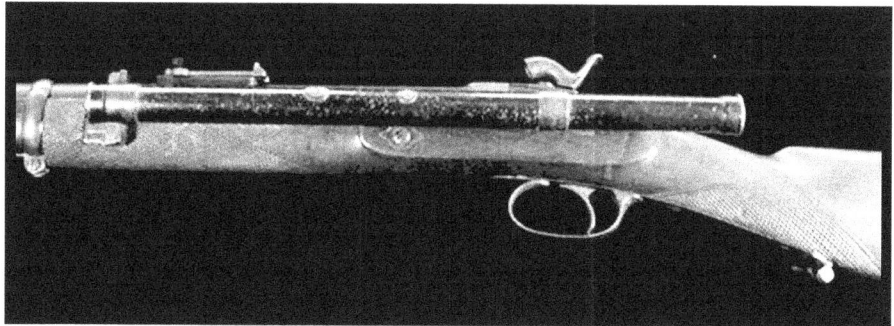

Variations of the Whitworth Rifle with Globe site (top & middle) and Telescopic Site (bottom). Private collection. Used with permission.

THE BATTLE OF HURRICANE BRIDGE, MARCH 28, 1863

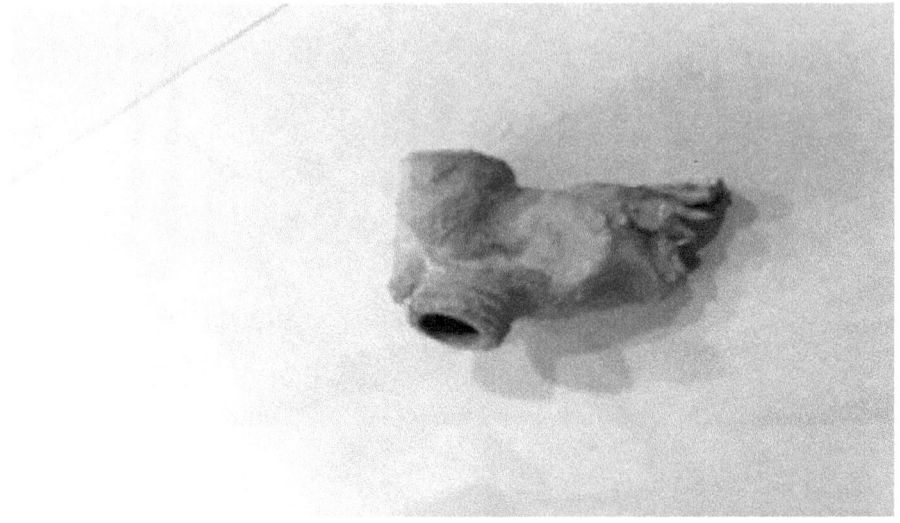

a. Whitworth .451 caliber bullet (11.5 mm diameter) recovered at Hurricane Bridge. The round struck a tree and expanded upon impact. This item is on display at the City of Hurricane office.

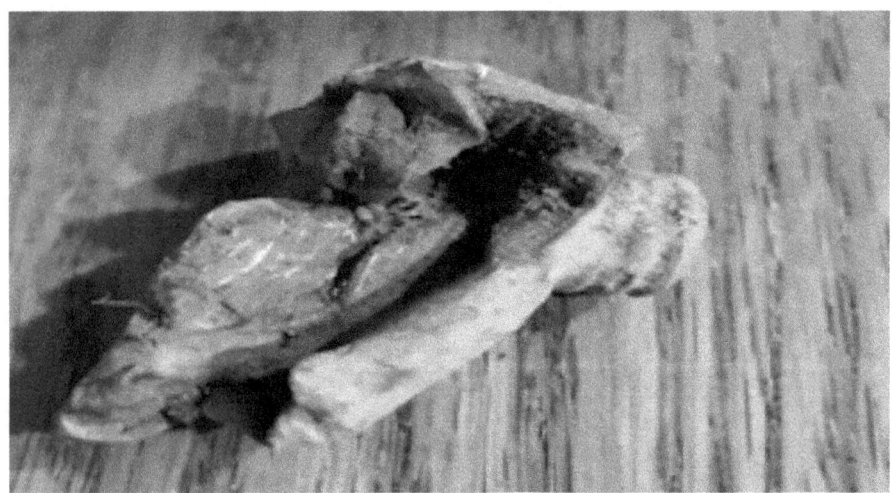

b. Side View of the above Whitworth .451 Bullet recovered at Hurricane Bridge. It takes little effort to imagine the damage such a bullet could do to a human body.

Using textbook firing maneuvers "fire by company" and "fire by ranks," Captain James Johnson directed his two flank companies, A on the right, and B on the left, respectively, to deliver a massed, deliberate fire against Jenkins' sharpshooters located on the eastern and southern heights some two to three hundred yards away. They were at an elevation of roughly one hundred fifty to three hundred yards higher than the troops massed along the ridge behind the tavern. The latter commands required an entire company of fifty or more men to fire simultaneously, shoulder to shoulder, in close ranks, toward a common target. The result was a condensed, massed line of fire pouring dozens of rounds into their foe and is tactically sound from Johnson's location, as opposed to random firing at such distance. In this fashion, Johnson knew he had a much better chance of eliminating as many of the dreaded sharpshooters as possible.[10]

Previous research speculated that Jenkins' men did not have infantry training and posited this was why he did not attack the Union position by frontal assault. However, several companies in Jenkins' battalion were formerly serving as infantry in 1861, and they spent the previous winter at Dublin, Virginia, learning the rudiments of infantry drill. There is also ample evidence they were fully armed and equipped as infantry in March 1863. However, only a few of Jenkins' officers, including Captain Jonathan Hankins of Company C, 16th Virginia Cavalry, were fully trained in both cavalry and infantry tactics. Hankins enlisted on May 29, 1861, at Tazewell, Virginia. He was elected captain of Company C in late 1862 and sent to the Officer's Camp of Instruction at Salem, Virginia, where he learned both infantry and cavalry tactics. He had only recently completed the training on January 15, 1863 and returned to his regiment and was yet inexperienced to confidently lead an infantry company in battle. Further, there is ample evidence Jenkins was fully armed and equipped his battalion with infantry equipment prior to leaving on this expedition.[11]

Another of Jenkins' officers was relatively new to his job, causing more concern about sending a massed infantry formation to attack the Union position. 1st Lieutenant Joel Abbott enlisted in the 8th Virginia Cavalry on May 5, 1862, at Giles County, Virginia and was appointed 2nd Lieutenant of Company H on May 14, 1862. On March 10, 1863, he was appointed 1st Lieutenant in the field; in other words, with no formal training as to the specifics of managing a company as 1st Lieutenant. In the Napoleonic tactical systems used during the Civil War, simple on-the-job training was usually insufficient to acquire such skill in a few days' time, as it required memorizing a difficult series of commands to maneuver a large, linear formation of troops through highly complex evolutions of the line in combat conditions. Abbott was promoted only two weeks prior to the battle at Hurricane Bridge on March 28, 1863; while his prior experience as 2nd Lieutenant was doubtless useful, it was not the same as required of a 1st Lieutenant. Abbott later transferred into Company K, 22nd Virginia Infantry in 1864.[12]

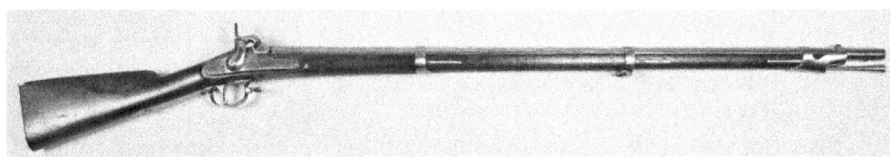

1842 U.S. Springfield Rifled Musket, .69 caliber and socket bayonet. Private Collection.

1861 Richmond Musket, Rifled, .69 caliber. Private Collection. Used with permission.

1862 Austrian Lorenz Rifle. Author's Collection.

Although the Union earth works were not finished, it they still afforded a reasonable degree of protection, and Union soldiers likely only had to expose their head and shoulder areas to fire for the most part, but there were clearly exceptions. Corporal Leroy Newman, Company H, was severely wounded in the right thigh as a musket ball passed through both legs, breaking his right femur (thigh bone). He was briefly treated at the field hospital and sent home afterward and did not return to duty. From all accounts, he never fully recovered and later filed a claim for a pension due to disability. Also, nineteen year-old private Henry Hoffman of Company D was "slightly wounded in the head" during the fighting that day. Hoffman was hospitalized at the Hurricane Bridge field hospital and returned to duty in May 1863.[13]

For the most part, the Confederates had to find small targets visible above the earth works which were unfinished, although a few soldiers on the southern heights likely managed to fire into the Federal right flank, a tactic known as "Enfilade" firing. This forced the sharpshooters and dismounted troopers to take careful, deliberate aim, rather than random firing as commonly occurred during the chaos of battle. It may also account for why the battle at Hurricane Bridge lasted for five hours. Sharpshooters tended to look for officers first, because wounding or killing them would increase the likelihood of chaos inside of the opposing lines.

They mortally wounded one officer in this fashion, twenty-one-year-old 1st Lieutenant Emory J. Bridgeman, who was initially in Company F in 1861. He later became the 13th West Virginia Adjutant, and he served in that role on March 28, 1863. He received multiple gunshot wounds inside the earthworks, and "poor Bridgeman" died in the Hurricane Bridge field hospital on March 31, 1863 according to Dr. Samuel G. Shaw. Bridgeman was five feet, ten inches tall, and hailed from Meigs County, Ohio. He also had light complexion, gray eyes, with light hair, and had worked as a clerk prior to the war. His personal effects were sent to his mother as his last request. Bridgeman's body was sent home also and is buried at Bridgeman Cemetery in Sutton Township, Meigs County, Ohio. The Civil War took a hard toll on his family, as his brother, Austin Bridgeman, who served in the 63rd Ohio Volunteer Infantry as a surgeon, was killed aboard the steamer Sultana when the engines exploded on April 27, 1865, killing 1,800 of the roughly 2,500 soldiers onboard, who were returning home. Known as the worst maritime disaster in the Civil War, the steamship traveled the Mississippi river and was rated maximum capacity for only 376 people.[14]

The loss of Lieutenant Emory Bridgeman took a hard toll on many men in the 13th West Virginia, as he was popular and well respected. Colonel Brown in particular was struck by his death but knew he had to promptly replace him. Brown wrote to Governor Francis Pierpont on April 15, 1863, from Hurricane Bridge, requesting the following: "Sir: I have the honor to request that you will commission Lieut. John S. Cunningham of the 11th Regt VA Vols as Adjutant of this Regiment in place of Emory J. Bridgeman, who was killed in action at Hurricane Bridge Va. Lieutenant Cunningham is the choice of the Officers of the Regiment, and I earnestly request that you commission him." Cunningham was appointed Adjutant of the 13th West Virginia Regiment on April 2, 1863. He was from Coalsmouth and was the son-in-law of wealthy attorney Samuel Benedict, who helped draft the new West Virginia state constitution in 1861. He enlisted in Captain John Valley Young's Company G early in 1861 and was a member of the 80th Regiment, Virginia Militia before that. Cunningham was quickly given a commission as 2nd Lieutenant, and he was known as a strict, but efficient, officer. He was charged with Conduct and Language Unbecoming an Officer and Gentleman on July 5, 1864, by a Sergeant Henry Farley of Company D, who was his subordinate.

According to the charges, Cunningham was frustrated with Sergeant Farley, who was routinely late on official company paperwork, raised his voice and swore at him with "disrespectful language" when he ordered him to pick up some blank forms needed for monthly reports, and the sergeant returned empty handed. Cunningham angrily told him that "Company D was an ass of a company and were behind in everything, and if you want to know the aggregate [total number of troops present] you can get it the best way you can for I do not concern myself about it." Charges were dropped, but his reputation was tarnished. Cunningham eventually resigned on January 10, 1865 and accepted a commission as Lieutenant-Colonel in the 80th Regiment West Virginia Militia in Kanawha County near his home. He cited concerns that his property was being stolen and damaged by Confederate guerillas, and for his family, whom he indicated were in persistent danger.[15]

Colonel William Brown summarized his casualties at Hurricane Bridge as follows: "…when the rebel force withdrew leaving 4 wounded who were taken prisoners. Our loss were 4 killed and 3 wounded." Captain Milton Stewart, Company B, reported "our loss three men killed, eight wounded…Company B lost two men killed in action." However, those reports conflict with other records, including the morning reports for Companies A, B, D and H of the 13th West Virginia Infantry on March 28, 1863. Rather, there were four wounded and three killed in action, and one man mortally wounded, (Adjutant 1st Lieutenant Emory Bridgeman) at Hurricane Bridge. One historian simply stated "several were killed," unable to resolve the matter.

Nineteen-year-old Corporal James [John] A. Rayburn, Company B, 13th West Virginia, was also "slightly wounded in the head in action" at Hurricane Bridge, attesting to the Confederates' marksmanship at such a distance posted behind earthen fortifications. He was taken to the field hospital and later examined by Dr. Samuel G. Shaw, who released him to duty. Rayburn was also a blacksmith and had been working in that capacity at Hurricane Bridge as "extra duty" during February and March. Rayburn was later captured at the battle of Cedar Creek on October 19, 1864 and incarcerated until the end of the war. The number of well-aimed shots in this action attests to both the Confederates' marksmanship and their use of technology, i.e. the Whitworth Globe sighted rifles. Others were not so fortunate as to survive their wounds; eighteen-year-old Private Jesse Hart of Company B died instantly from a gunshot wound at Hurricane Bridge. He enlisted on August 9, 1862 at Point Pleasant. He was a resident of Dutch Flats in Mason County. His height was five feet, nine inches, and he had a light complexion, blue eyes and light hair. His personal effects and extra uniform items were given to a friend in Company D.

John S. Cunningham, Post-War image.
West Virginia State Archives.

Grave marker of Private Henry Sands, Mace Cemetery, Big Chimney, West Virginia. Photo by Jared Cunningham.

A Confederate bullet also found Private Henry Sands of Company A, who was twenty-five years old. His brother, Matthew Sands, served in the 8th West Virginia Infantry and was stationed at Bull Town on March 28, 1863. They were both friends with Captain Edgar Blundon, who commanded Company F of the 8th West Virginia and several soldiers in both regiments. Captain Blundon wrote to his fiancée, Ms. Sarah Young of Coalsmouth, on April 16 that his men were "indignant" toward Jenkins when they learned of Sands' death at Hurricane Bridge. Sands' body was recovered by family and later buried at the Mace Cemetery in Big Chimney, West Virginia. Private Altimus Young, of Company B, was also killed in action at Hurricane Bridge on March 28, 1863. He was then eighteen years old and a resident of Point Pleasant, where he enlisted on October 18, 1862. Young stood 5'11" tall, with dark hair and eyes and a dark complexion, and he worked as a farmer prior to the war. Young's body was sent home to Mason County and buried in Greer Cemetery.[16] (Appendix G)

THE BATTLE OF HURRICANE BRIDGE, MARCH 28, 1863

There were no casualties reported in the 16th Virginia Cavalry at Hurricane Bridge. As was common in the Civil War, there were discrepancies in Union and Confederate casualty reports. For example, Captain James W. Johnson of the 13th West Virginia cited that "a few" wounded Confederates were captured, while Confederate records indicate there was one man killed and two men wounded, and both were captured. Sergeant James D. Sedinger of Company D, 8th Virginia Cavalry also wrote in his diary that there was one man from his company killed, whom he identified as Private John Payne of Company E. Payne enlisted on April 30, 1861, at Giles Court House, Virginia. It is presumed the body was buried in the vicinity of the battlefield at Hurricane Bridge, since Jenkins left his casualties on the field. If so, the grave is unmarked.

One historian stated there were two men killed in action and "several" men wounded at Hurricane Bridge. Muster rolls identify only one man, John R. Chapman, of Company D, 8th Virginia Cavalry, who was reported as "killed in Putnam County in 1863." However, service records indicated he was captured in Logan County on April 24, 1864, and sent to Athenaeum Prison at Wheeling, and then to Camp Chase, Ohio. Chapman was later hospitalized at Jackson Hospital in Richmond during March 1865 and diagnosed with debilitas on March 5, 1863. He was given a thirty-day furlough on March 8, 1863 and presumed to have remained home until the end of the war as there is no evidence he returned to his unit.

Two of Jenkins' wounded at Hurricane Bridge were relatives from the same extended family in Cabell County. Private Thomas H. Morris of Company D suffered a gunshot wound and was captured "at the same time" as Jordan Morris at Hurricane Bridge. Thomas was aged forty-four years and was employed as a minister prior to the war. Enlisting on September 4, 1862, at Cabell County, the 1860 United States Census indicates he left his wife and seven children at home to serve in the army. He was not a slave owner and held property valued at $200.00. Jordan T.[C] Morris, who was aged twenty-two-years, was also "wounded at Hurricane Bridge and left at that place." Thomas was afterward listed as "in the hands of the enemy" on Company D records. Both men received medical care by Dr. Samuel G. Shaw at the Hurricane Bridge field hospital, until taken to prison at Camp Chase, Ohio in May 1863.

They were moved to Fort Delaware, Maryland, in August and later transferred to Point Lookout in 1864. Jordan Morris died from acute dysentery there on January 28, 1865. Jordan Morris was five feet, six inches tall, with gray eyes, dark hair and a "florid" complexion. While it seems reasonable to infer these two men were of the same family, 1850 and 1860 census did not show the exact family relationship of Thomas and Jordan; Thomas is shown, but Jordan is not on either record, and military documents identified him as a resident of Cabell County. Because Captain Johnson of the 13th West Virginia indicated there were "a few" wounded Confederates, it is quite likely there were more, although military records do not identify them.[17]

Fighting lasted for five hours at Hurricane Bridge, with minimal casualties for each side. This was unusual during the Civil War, considering the amount of ammunition expended in the affair with rifled muskets. There were several reasons for this, not the least of which was the distance between the units engaged, and a shroud of heavy smoke surrounding the Union fort, which forced Jenkins' sharpshooters posted on the opposite heights to be slow and deliberate when aiming their muskets. Another factor was the earthen-fort; although yet unfinished, the fort still provided a great deal of protection for the Union troops, making them less visible. Also, the 13th West Virginia soldiers were relatively inexperienced. This was their first combat experience as a cohesive regiment, and while they were well disciplined, most of the officers had never commanded a company or battalion in an open battle not involving bushwhackers. This likely added to the inherent battle confusion at Hurricane Bridge, although they ultimately managed a very effective defense of their post. The Confederates, on the other hand, were physically exhausted and hungry, and many were without shoes. The weather had been rainy and quite cold, and the ground was still muddy also, making it difficult to maintain an aggressive posture.

Captain James Johnson's stubborn defense of Hurricane Bridge eventually led Jenkins to withdraw. Around 11:00 a.m., Jenkins realized he was not able to capture the Union garrison, and quietly withdrew behind the hills located to the south. Using the hills as a screen, the Confederates retreated westward, flanking the Federal position. Once out of range from Federal fire, Jenkins continued on the James River Turnpike.

Captain Johnson was proud of his men and reported they had withstood the heavy, galling crossfire and "...returned with the firmness of veterans." Johnson's official report of the action states, "The enemy sharpshooters were so posted on the adjacent heights and armed with globe sighted rifles were constantly endeavoring to pick off officers and men. After five hours of brisk and animated firing from both sides the enemy suddenly withdrew his forces leaving few of his wounded who fell into our hands. From whom we learned that the enemy force engaged did not number less than 500 men. Our loss was 3 killed and 4 wounded, one of whom has since died. To both officers and men, I return my most sincere thanks for the bravery and gallantry displayed during the engagement where so many heroic deeds were performed; it would be unjust to mention individual acts of gallantry. It is enough to say that they all behaved in the most noble and gallant manner."[18]

Before leaving Hurricane Bridge, however, the Confederates burned several houses and buildings, including the log structure used as a church and school. In the annals of warfare, civilians inevitably suffer loss of either life, property, or both when the opposing armies are nearby. It is not known whether Jenkins authorized the homes burnt, or whether some of his men engaged in it on their own. While speculative, it is not a foregone conclusion that since approximately eighty-one men from the immediate vicinity of Hurricane Bridge enlisted there in May 1861, and were doubtless familiar with the residents, that many were well aware who the numerous Union supporters were and settled personal vendettas against them. While no civilian casualties were reported at Hurricane Bridge, the loss of their homes and church caused about twenty-four residents to scatter, including John and Rachel Griffith, the parents of Private Lewis Griffith of Company G, 13th West Virginia.

Griffith was at that time stationed at nearby Coalsmouth and did not likely hear of his family circumstances until a few days later. John and Rachel Griffith were also founding members of the Baptist Church group that met at Hurricane Bridge. That church did not resume meetings there until 1871, when they erected a log frame building on the southeastern corner of the land, where the modern First Baptist Church of Hurricane is located. On April 2, 1877, the fellowship received a deed for the property purchased from Collis P. Huntington, President of the Central Land Company. Huntington was later responsible for orchestrating the new railroad system running through West Virginia to the Ohio River, and the modern city of Huntington, West Virginia is his namesake.[19]

Meanwhile, Jenkins turned his battalion northward along Benedict Road, went about one mile, and turned east. His next steps are not clear, but he likely crossed the dividing ridge line near Coon Creek or followed Poindexter until he came to Hurricane Creek. Then, he continued east toward his primary objective, the Union supply depot at Point Pleasant. Enroute, an incident supposedly occurred that is part of the local oral tradition, cited by Mrs. Irene Ambler of Putnam County in the May 7, 1987, issue of the *Hurricane Breeze* newspaper as follows: "Mr. Elmer Foster, a respected friend of mine, told me in the 1950's that his father saw the band of ragged Confederates with their wounded thrown across horses' backs marching down Hurricane Creek Road near Poindexter Road. Mr. Foster said, his father said, that one soldier slipped from the horse's back and rolled down the bank of Hurricane Creek, appearing to be dead. He said others picked him up and laid him again across the back of the horse." They then continued on their way, moving slowly down Hurricane Creek.[20]

As was common for many soldiers in the Civil War, twenty-eight-year-old Martin van Buren Edens of Company A, 13th West Virginia, memorialized the Battle at Hurricane Bridge in a poem. This was something commonly found in soldier diaries, letters home and occasionally local newspapers. Edens enlisted as a private on August 15, 1862, at Charleston, West Virginia. He was promoted to Corporal on September 23, 1862, and then reduced to the ranks (private) on June 1, 1864. He was severely wounded on September 19, 1864, at the Battle of Winchester and hospitalized at Chester, Virginia, until transferred to the army hospital at Gallipolis, Ohio, a few weeks later, where he remained until the end of the war.[21]

THE BATTLE OF HURRICANE BRIDGE, MARCH 28, 1863

A Soldier's Poem: Skirmish at Hurricane Bridge!

Between a high hill and circuitous ridge,
Is the neat little town, known as Hurricane Bridge,
Or at least, 'twas a neat little village before -
The rebellion arose in the bright days of yore.
But rebellion has banished those pleasures, so sweet,
And the wail of despair is now heard in the street –

The many fine buildings in ashes are laid
The wealth of the inmates forever decayed.
The 13th Virginia is camped near this town,
Who in a late battle have won great renown.
The regiment is formed of a brave set of boys,
Who accomplish their work without making much noise.

But Albert G. Jenkins not aware of that fact,
Came early one morning to make an attack,
With a yard of white cotton unfurled to the breeze,
His staff came into camp, while Jenkins stayed behind trees.

'Twas Samuels who brought in the banner of truce.
Says Johnson, to surrender I this morning refuse.
In the time which is given to my works I'll repair.
And give you a battle on principles fair.
When cool as an iceberg we fell into line.
To defend the bright stars which on our banner doth shine,

And to hold our position at Hurricane Bridge,
In spite of the Rebs on each neighboring ridge.
For Jenkins marched forth with his menacing host
To capture or drive us away from our post,
He threw his men round on the top of each hill
To make us surrender or fly at his will.
He thought with his men on the left and the right,
He would capture our squad without having to fight

And with Yankee clothing he his men would equip,
And thus would secure successful his trip.
But Albert was much disappointed to find
To surrender that morning we were not inclined
Then he told all his men to prepare for the blow
And soon they'd conquer the insolent foe.

BATTLE AT HURRICANE BRIDGE MARCH 28, 1863

From each hill top they fired on the 13th in vain,
For each at his post did boldly remain.

For the space of four hours he fought very hard
But his incessant firing we not much did regard.
Like Jeff. Davis' scrip that's more plenty than good,
They sent in their lead from each neighboring wood
Like the insects that sing in the long days of June,
The balls from the Rebs almost whistled a tune,

But it was not sufficient to induce us to dance,
It was like Mason in England or Slidell in France,
Who after they made known their treacherous plan,
Have to end their hard labor just where they began.
With stomach's quite empty and feet without shoes,
Each felt like a bankrupt with a spell of the blues,

Like a dishonored guest ere the banquet is o'er
Arrives at the feast and is kept from the door.
They knew in our camp were crackers, coffee and meat,
And they longed to get in to get something to eat.
Like Cruse's man Friday, who on the mountain did stand,
And beheld in the distance, his own native land.

With obstacles in front which he could not surmount
Was not able to settle the lengthy account,
And fell ere he crossed o'er the dark rolling wave
And found in the deep sea a watery grave.

So Jenkins after giving us a hard shower of hail
And finding with muskets he could not prevail
Sent out his command to retreat from the field,
For the 13th Virginia was too stubborn to yield.

Being tired and hungry, they left in disgust,
Aware of the fact that Albert won't do to trust;
He promised to give them both food and attire,
In short everything that a reb could desire.

Except a good thrashing they left as they came
With nothing to brighten Jeff. Davis' fame;
And Jenkins found out that one blunder he made
In seeking for sunshine he found naught but shade.[22]

THE BATTLE OF HURRICANE BRIDGE, MARCH 28, 1863

Bullets recovered at Hurricane Bridge. The larger ball on the left is a Grape Shot. There was no artillery in the March 28, 1863, battle; this was likely dropped or fell off of a supply train passing through the area. The bullet in the middle is a .58 caliber Minié ball, a standar round of both Union and Confederate armies. On the right is a .6 caliber Minié ball, also used in the Richmond Rifled Muskets by Jenkins' troopers and the 13th West Virginia at Hurricane Bridge.

.58 Caliber Minié Ball recovered near Hurricane Bridge. Courtesy Brett Kirby.

Part of a horseshoe recovered in Union camp area near Hurricane Bridge. Courtesy Brett Kirby.

Rivet with leather attached recovered in Union camp area near Hurricane Bridge. Likely came from a Union Knapsack; the 1858 Pattern Knapsacks issued to Federal soldiers in 1861-1865 commonly employed these items. Courtesy Brett Kirby.

Lead bar recovered in Union camp area near Hurricane Bridge.
Soldiers commonly melted these to use in bullet molds. Courtesy Brett Kirby.

Axe head recovered in Union camp area near Hurricane Bridge.
Courtesy Brett Kirby.

Bullets recovered at Hurricane Bridge. Bottom right and top left are Whitworth .45 caliber. Others are .69 and .58 caliber Minie' balls; Enfield .577 Caliber and a .69 caliber "Pumpkin ball" used in smooth bore arms. Courtesy Nathan Easter.

Chapter Six References

1. Conner, 6-8.
2. Miller O.R. Skirmish at Hurricane Bridge; Hurricane Centennial, 4-5; Brownlee, Kimberly Ball Hieronimus. The Thirteenth Regiment, West Virginia Volunteer Infantry. Unpublished Senior Thesis, University of Toledo, 1996. Call No. 973.7454. WV State Archives, 6-7. (Hereafter Brownlee, 13th WV); Dickinson, *8th Virginia Cavalry*, 28; 37-38; Johnson, Flora. S. The Civil War Record of Albert Gallatin Jenkins, C.S.A. *West Virginia History*. (July 1947). Vol. 8(4), 392-404.
3. James B. Wiggins Papers, 1861-1919. Virginia Sesquicentennial of the American Civil War Collection, Call Number 44358, Manuscripts, Library of Virginia; Miller, O.R. Skirmish at Hurricane Bridge; 13th WV Field History, Part 1 and Appendix A; OR, Series 1, Vol. 19, p. 1083.
4. Sedinger Diary, 55-78; Dickinson, *16th Virginia* Cavalry; Edens, Battle of Hurricane Bridge; CSR, 8th Virginia Cavalry, RG 94, M324, roll 85; CSR, 13th West Virginia Infantry, M508, Roll 205, National Archives.
5. Hess John H. Civil War Letters, February 18 and April 10, 1863. Author's Collection: CSR, 13th West Virginia, RG 94, M508, Rolls 204 & 209, National Archives; 13th West Virginia Morning Reports, Company B, March 28, 1863.
6. 13th WV Field History, Part 1 and Appendix A; OR, Series 1, Vol. 19, 1083; Miller, O.R. Skirmish at Hurricane Bridge; Sedinger Diary, 55-78; Edens, Battle of Hurricane Bridge.
7. Dupuy, Trevor N. *The Evolution of Weapons and Warfare*. (Boston, MA: DaCapo Press, 1900); Whisker, James B. *U.S. and Confederate Arms and Armories During the American Civil War: Arms Imported from Europe During the American Civil War, 1861-1865*. (Lewiston, NY: E. Mellen Press, 2002), OR, Series 1, Vol. 25, Part 2, 657-658.
8. Civil War Letters of Thomas P. Copenshaver, 8th Virginia Cavalry. Stuart A. Rose Library Manuscript and Archives, MSS-20, Emory University, Atlanta Georgia; Dr. Shaw Letters, April 6, 1863; 13th West Virginia Infantry Morning Reports, October 15, 1862, Company A received a shipment of 1862 Austrian Lorenz Rifles.
9. CSR, 13th West Virginia, RG 94, M508, Roll 205, National Archives; WV AG Papers, 13th West Virginia, AR 382, Box 23, Company H Muster Rolls, WV State Archives.

10. Hardee, William J. *1855 Manual for Rifle and Light Infantry Tactics. 1861 Revised edition*. Parts 1 and 4. (Philadelphia, PA: Lippincott Publishing, 1861). Original volumes in author's collection.
11. CSR, 16th Virginia Cavalry, M324, Rolls 146 & 147, National Archives.
12. "Another Sheriff Captured." *Wheeling Intelligencer*, February 21, 1863. Written by unidentified 13 WV soldier on February 11, 1863. Library of Congress; CSR, 8th Virginia Cavalry, RG 94, M324, Roll 81, National Archives.
13. Hardee, William J. *Rifle and Light Infantry Tactics: For Exercise and Manoeuvres of Troops When Acting as Light Infantry or Riflemen*. Volume 1. (New York: J.O. Kane, Publisher, 1862). Original copy in author's collection; Sedinger Diary, 55-78; 13th WV Field History, Part 1 and Appendix A; OR, Series 1, Vol. 19, 1083; Hurricane Centennial, 4-5; CSR, Union Service Records, 13th West Virginia, RG 94, M508, Roll 207, National Archives; WV AG, Union Regiments, 13th West Virginia, AR 382, Box 20, Muster Roll April 10, 1863, WV State Archives; *West Virginia Adjutant General's Report*. December 1, 1864. (Wheeling, WV: J.F. M'Dermot Publishing, 1864), 364-366; 13th West Virginia Infantry Morning Reports, Co.'s A-D, F-K, February –March 1863.
14. CSR, 13th West Virginia, RG 94, M506 Roll 204, National Archives; Dr. Shaw Letters, March 31, 1863; WV AG Papers, 13th West Virginia, AR 382, Box 20, Muster Roll April 10, 1863, WV State Archives; See also: Potter, Jerry. The Sultana Tragedy: America's Greatest Maritime Disaster. (Baton Rouge, LA: Pelican Publishing, 1992).
15. WV AR, AR 382, Union Regiments, 13th West Virginia, Box 20, Folder 1, WV State Archives. Griffith, pp. 8-9. CSR, 13th West Virginia, RG 94, M508, Roll 204, National Archives.
16. 13th West Virginia Field History, Part 1; OR, Series 1, Vol. CSR, 13th West Virginia, RG 94, M507-M508, Rolls 204, 206, 208, 209 and 211, National Archives; WV AG Papers, Union Regiments, 13th West Virginia, AR 382, Box 20, Muster Roll April 10, 1863, WV State Archives; Comstock, p. 131; Blundon Letters, April 16, 1863.
17. Dickinson, *8th Virginia Cavalry*, 33-37, 77; Dickinson, 16th Virginia Cavalry, 18; 13th WV Field History, Part 1, Appendix A; CSR, 8th Virginia Cavalry, RG 94, M324, Rolls 81-86, National Archives; 1860 US Census.
18. *Hurricane Centennial*, 5-6.
19. Griffith, 69-70.

20. 13th West Virginia Field History, Part 1, Appendix A; Miller, OR, Series 1, Vol. 51, Part 1, 176; Miller, O.R. Skirmish at Hurricane Bridge; Griffith, 70; Dickinson, J.L. & Summer-Ramirez, Alison K., Historic Huntington Businesses: The Birth of Huntington, W.Va. 1871-1900. 2016. Unpublished Manuscript. Huntington, WV: Marshall University Libraries, 9-12.

21. 13th West Virginia Field History, Part 1; CSR, 8th Virginia Cavalry, RG 94, M324, Roll 205, National Archives.

22. Edens, Battle of Hurricane Bridge.

Chapter Seven

JENKINS ATTACKS AT POINT PLEASANT MARCH 30, 1863

Companies C, E and F of the 13th West Virginia were at Point Pleasant on March 28, 1863; upon hearing of the attack at Hurricane Bridge later that day, Brigadier General Eliakim P. Scammon ordered Colonel Brown to send Companies C and F on a forced march to Hurricane Bridge to assist Captain Johnson's four companies, a distance of more than fifty miles. They arrived around 4:00 PM the next day, only to find Jenkins was long gone. Company E then remained at Point Pleasant under the command of Captain John D. Carter, with sixty men present for duty. This company was originally recruited as an independent sharpshooter company in August 1862, but that organization "never was finished" according to Private George Rucker. General Jacob D. Cox thought Captain Carter had around two hundred fifty men present, but Colonel William Brown later reported he only had about sixty men there and estimated Jenkins had around four hundred men. Later that day, Cox realized, "The force at Point Pleasant is weaker than I supposed, General Scammon had ordered most of it to sustain the post at Hurricane Bridge and only one company is left there."[1]

After abandoning the attack at Hurricane Bridge, Jenkins took a circuitous route toward Point Pleasant via Hurricane Creek and bivouacked that night near the Kanawha River. On March 29, 1863, Jenkins' cavalrymen were still marching through Putnam County toward Point Pleasant; they encountered two Union steamers, *Victor No. 2* and *General Meigs* at Hallo Landing near Frazier's Bottom; *Victor No. 2* was carrying an Army paymaster, Major B.R. Cowen, and some soldiers along with several thousand dollars in cash. The boat was moving down river, and a small group of Confederates were sent to the shore while the remainder hid themselves among trees and bushes, while a local farm hand flagged the ship down, pretending to be a potential passenger.. A local farm hand pretending flag the ship down. When the steamer drew near, Jenkins ordered his men to fire across the bow, hoping to capture both steamers, but failed, killing one man and one horse and wounding one man and several horses on the *Victor No. 2*. Instead of surrendering, Captain Ford ordered full speed ahead and hunkered down behind the wheel, as a hail of bullets riddled the ship, shattering the glass in the wheelhouse. Ford proceeded to Point Pleasant and managed to warn Captain John Carter, Company E, 13th West Virginia of Jenkins' approach.[2]

Putnam County resident Fred Conner wrote of the incident,

...the steamer *Victor No. 2* commanded by Cap. Fred Ford...having on board the paymaster B. R. Cowen in whose possession was a large amount of government funds. When opposite the landing she was hailed by an individual who was apparently alone, the command being concealed behind a clump of trees. The boat rounded in, when reaching the shore she received fire from a heretofore concealed force. Cap. Ford ordered the steamer to be backed and thus she escaped capture, but not before she was pretty thoroughly riddled with balls...[3]

A Point Pleasant resident who witnessed the damage to the *Victor No. 2* editorialized the following in the Gallipolis Journal on April 9, 1863:

JENKINS ATTACKS AT POINT PLEASANT MARCH 30, 1863

No loyal citizen can look at the effect of the murderous fire poured into the Government steamboat *Victor No. 2*, by Jenkins' brigade on the Kanawha...without saying how narrowly our town escaped destruction, and how many happy homes might now be the scene of desolation and mourning....every bullet hole in the boat conveys an idea of terrible import. That they designed to capture but not destroy the boat, is evident in the fact that the fire was directed from and not at the machinery of the boat. They knew that a shot in the steam heater or pipes would effectually deprive them of using her as a transport. When captured, to steam directly to Gallipolis was the work of a few hours. Point Pleasant would then have probably escaped plunder, not from choice but from fear of giving the citizens of Gallipolis notice of their danger. No one can deny that in case of capture, the boat loaded with the enemy might have landed at our wharf unmolested, and commenced their work of destruction before any effort could be made to oppose them...[4]

Another citizen of Point Pleasant bluntly recalled,

Only by contemplating the probable results of a surrender, can we properly estimate the value of the services rendered by the intrepid Captain. [Capt. Frederick Ford] Had he, to insure safety, given up his boat, the enemy would have filled her with troops, and all things being in readiness, made a descent upon this place-then all unsuspecting of danger-taken by surprise, our little band of soldiers...burned the rest of the government stores...and, if not appraised of their approach, would doubtless have burned that flourishing town...Well may we shudder, in reflecting how imminent was destruction...[5]

Meanwhile on March 29, 1863, Jenkins moved northward along the Kanawha River, and further upriver discovered two other boats, embarked, and then proceeded down the river to Point Pleasant. Arriving there on the morning of March 30, 1863, Jenkins found some sixty men from Company E, 13th West Virginia and approximately one hundred soldiers from the nearby army hospital waiting for them.

Sergeant J.D. Sedinger, Company D, 8th Virginia Cavalry, recalled, "... We flanked the fort and moved that day to Buffalo on the Kanawha River, captured two flat boats, went aboard and floated down the Kanawha to Point Pleasant, went ashore and charged the town."[6]

Jenkins attacked at 11:00 A.M. on March 30, 1863, but after that point details are somewhat conflicted. According to one source, "... around 11 o'clock. At that time, Captain John D. Carter, commanding Company E, 13th Virginia Regiment, (Federal), was encamped two squares above the courthouse, and when the firing began, which was the first intimations of the presence of the Confederates, they fled into the courthouse for refuge. Here they were closely besieged for four hours, during which time a desultory fire was kept up on both sides. Jenkins found not only Company E guarding the garrison and supply depot, but after the fighting continued into the afternoon, Sergeant J.D. Sedinger of the 8th Virginia Cavalry noted "The enemy reinforced from Gallipolis..."[7]

Around 3:00 P.M., a group of home guards and militia entered the fight, having with them was a three gun battery of artillery, which at once prepared to shell the town, "...thinking that the Confederates, instead of the Federals, occupied the court-house, but this impression was corrected in time to save the town."

One of those units was "The Trumble Guards", from Gallipolis in Warren County, commanded by Colonel Charles W. Smith who had around fifty men. Another home guard unit stationed there on March 28, 1863 was the "Squirrel Hunters", also from Warren County with about fifty-five men. Warren County boasted ties to several Union officers in the Civil War, including General Cox, who had also served as Superintendent of Warren County Schools before the war, and Robert K. Ratliff, a Union soldier who helped capture Confederate President Jefferson Davis in 1865.[8]

Most sources indicate that Company E and the home guards eventually repulsed the Jenkins raiders after nearly three hours of intense fighting in the streets of the town; however, General Jacob D. Cox, who was in Marietta, Ohio at the time, reported that Captain Carter's Company E were already inside the Court House and had sent for help, but expressed confidence in Carter's ability to defend the post, erroneously thinking he had two hundred fifty men on hand to fight. Major General

Robert S. Schenck, commanding Middle Military Department (which then included western Virginia) said he received a telegram on March 30, 1863, from General Cox at 2:00 P.M. stating, "The company at Point Pleasant was, at 11 a.m., still in the courthouse, and hoped to hold it till night. I have directed the commander at Gallipolis to raise volunteers of the citizens there, and endeavor to relieve the garrison. Have also a boat to go down from Gallipolis for a regiment. Fifth Virginia, lately at Ceredo, and bring it, unless it has its hands full there..." J.D. Sedinger of the 8th Virginia Cavalry indicated simply that after some fighting, "The Yanks got possession of the Court House and we held the jail. Ed Gutherie was badly wounded, Lieutenant's Samuels and Holderby both taken prisoner..."[9]

Sedinger refers to Private Edward S. Gutherie, Company E, 8th Virginia Cavalry, who enlisted on April 20, 1862 at Giles Court House, Virginia. Gutherie was aged twenty-two years, a resident of Mason County, and stood 5'10" tall, with fair complexion, dark hair and brown eyes. He was a farmer prior to the war. Guthrie apparently had a bad habit of getting too close to enemy troops in the many small skirmishes he participated in during the war; he was not only wounded at Point Pleasant and captured there but was also formerly captured at Jumping Branch in Mercer County on February 9, 1862. Taken to Camp Chase, Ohio until October 31, 1862 when he was exchanged, he then returned to his regiment. Guthrie returned to Camp Chase following capture at Point Pleasant and recovered from a gunshot wound there. He was later transferred to Fort Delaware Maryland on March 4, 1864, and there remained until June 20, 1865, when he was released nearly two months after the war ended.[10]

Sedinger also mentioned Lieutenant twenty-four-year-old George W. Holderby of Company E. Holderby had enlisted on April 20, 1862 at Giles Court House, and he was earlier wounded in the battle of Lewisburg, West Virginia on May 23, 1862. Both he and Lieutenant Alexander Samuels were captured by the Trumbull Guards at Point Pleasant, although he was sent to Fort McHenry instead of Camp Chase with Samuels. Holderby was a resident of Cabell County, stood 6'1" tall, with gray eyes, light hair and fair complexion, and he had worked as a merchant prior to the war. He transferred to Fort McHenry in Maryland on April 20, 1863. Fort McHenry was where the National Anthem, "The

Star-Spangled Banner" was penned during the War of 1812. He was only there overnight, as he again transferred to Fort Norfolk on April 21, 1863 and stayed an indefinite period of time. He returned to duty, however, and was again captured at Guyandotte on April 28, 1864 and taken to Camp Chase, until February 25, 1865, when he was sent to City Point Virginia until the end of the war.[11]

Lieutenant Alexander Samuels was the officer who had carried the Flag of Truce to Captain James W. Johnson of the 13th West Virginia at Hurricane Bridge on March 28, 1863. He was imprisoned at Athenaeum Prison in Wheeling on April 3, 1863. He was sent to Fort McHenry on April 19, 1863 and transferred to Fort Monroe on April 10, 1863. Next, he was sent to Fort Norfolk on April 21, 1863 and paroled shortly afterward. He was killed while on patrol in the Kanawha Valley on January 3, 1864. His body was found by staff officers from General John S. Williams, commanding 2nd Brigade, of the Kanawha, on whose staff Samuels also briefly served before his death. In addition, Dr. Charles Timmons, the surgeon who traveled with Jenkins' staff, stayed behind after the battle to care for the wounded and was captured and sent to the Union prison at Wheeling.[12]

> During the fighting at Point Pleasant, one of the most execrable acts of the war occurred. This was the shooting of the venerable Colonel Andrew Waggener, who was aged eighty-four years, by a Confederate soldier. He was riding toward Point Pleasant on Crooked Creek Road and carrying his cane, when he was met by the soldier, who halted him and demanded his horse. He refused to give it up, upon which the soldier attempted to take hold of the reins, when the Colonel attempted to strike him with his cane. The soldier then stepped back and shot him dead. The act was condemned in the strongest terms by General Jenkins afterward.[13]

Major General Robert C. Schenck informed Governor Francis Pierpont via a telegram dated March 30, 1863 that "we are driving them" and expected Union troops to have Point Pleasant cleared of Confederates shortly; however, there is also no other evidence Schenck was at Point Pleasant when Jenkins attacked. Colonel William Brown opined that Jenkins ultimately realized "they could not take the place" and retreated around 3:30 P.M., sustaining a loss of seventy-six men killed, wounded and prisoners, including six officers. Brown stated, "Our own loss was two killed and three wounded, including 1st Lieutenant William N. Hawkins," who was seriously wounded in the shoulder; however, Hawkins actually received a gunshot wound that pierced both lungs, but he later recovered. In spite of the inconsistencies in reports, it is clear, however, that during the fighting, the Trumble Guards captured one of Jenkins' officers, 1st Lieutenant Alexander H. Samuels of Company D, 8th Virginia Cavalry.[14]

Ultimately, the Confederates being disappointed in not taking or destroying all of the anticipated army stores and despairing of not being able to dislodge the Federals, withdrew, crossed the Kanawha and that night encamped on the headwaters of the Ohio River. The next morning they began marching toward Tazewell County, Virginia. After Jenkins withdrew from Point Pleasant, Sergeant J.D. Sedinger recalled the Confederates' next move: "…we left the town and fell back up the river to the mouth of 10 Mile, crossed the Kanawha and marched to Howell's Mill in Cabell County where we went into camp. The infantry and cavalry from Charleston undertook to cut us off but failed. We then resumed our march back to Dixie where we found our horses awaiting us in good condition."[15]

Brigadier General Albert G. Jenkins. Library of Congress.

Captain John D. Carter, Co. E, 13th West Virginia Volunteer Infantry. West Virginia State Archives.

2nd Lieutenant Charles T. Latham, Co. E, 13th West Virginia Volunteer Infantry.
Courtesy St. Albans Historical Society, J.S. Cunningham Collection.

Colonel Rutherford B. Hayes, 23rd Ohio Volunteer Infantry. Hayes later became the Nineteenth President of the United States in 1877. West Virginia State Archives.

2nd Lieutenant John H. Rosler, Co. E, 13th West Virginia Volunteer Infantry. West Virginia State Archives.

1st Lieutenant William N. Hawkins, Co. E, 13th West Virginia Volunteer Infantry. West Virginia State Archives.

THE BATTLE OF HURRICANE BRIDGE, MARCH 28, 1863

Afterward, General Robert Schenck received Captain John Carter's report of the attack a few days later on April 4, 1863; he summarized,

> ...Captain Carter had 60 men. He reports 2 killed, 3 wounded, and 6 taken prisoners, making our total loss 11. The rebels lost, in killed, wounded and prisoners, 72, and so their raid, with their largely superior numbers, was handsomely repulsed. Under the orders given by General Scammon, I hope to hear that the enemy has been intercepted, and something more than hurried in his retreat.[16]

Captain Carter's official report is lost to history; however, local newspapers reported that he had not provided much resistance when the battle began and was with insufficient troops to manage an attack. Carter then sent a rebuttal to the editor of the *Weekly Register*, on April 6, 1863, describing the action at Point Pleasant as follows:

> In your issue of April 1st, 1863, you say: 'The same gang that fired into the steamers *Victor No. 2*, and *Gen. Meigs*, attacked Point Pleasant under command of Major Samuels, and that there were only some 30 men of the 13th Va. V.I. at Point Pleasant.' I wish to correct those statements, First the rebels were under the command of the 'invincible A.G. Jenkins', and not of Major Samuels, as you say. Second, you say there was no resistance shown to their entering the town, except from the Court-house; this is untrue. There was resistance shown in the streets before we entered the Court-house. There was enough soldiers in Pt. Pleasant to whip the rebels, which they did before help arrived. It is true the heavy ordnance came up on the Ohio side of the river; that the first act which the men in command of the artillery did was range their course for the Court-house and was only prevented from firing upon us by the earnest entreaty of some of the citizens of Point Pleasant who happened to be on that side of the river.
>
> While I admire the courage of the artillerymen, I think they exhibited devilish poor judgment, in their first attempt. You say that when the re-enforcements arrived on the Virginia side of the river there were only thirty of the enemy in sight: that is true.

JENKINS ATTACKS AT POINT PLEASANT MARCH 30, 1863

As to the shells from the artillery which caused so much consternation among the enemy it was not owing to the destruction they caused, for they fell short, (as some of your citizens can testify;) the noise may have scared the Rebs some. I award great credit to the Trumble Guards, and citizens who, did cross to our assistance, notwithstanding the enemy had retreated, for they crossed as soon as they could.

The steamer was detained for a reason that I will not now explain, but which I will, if any are curious to know, at a future time. And I will take this occasion to thank the soldiers and citizens of Gallipolis who did come to our relief. I thank you gentlemen, soldiers and citizens in the name of Company E, 13th Va. V.I. and will say, also, if you ever get into trouble, we will not be slow to your rescue. We know that your will was good to come to our assistance sooner; but we know you had no means to cross the river, unless you had swum it."[17]

As with most battles in the Civil War, local papers were flooded with editorials following the engagement; many reported conflicting information or that which was inconsistent with accounts provided from military sources. The following opinion appeared in the *Gallipolis Journal* on April 2, 1863, regarding the late attack on Point Pleasant:

On Monday at 12 M., word came to Gallipolis that the notorious Jenkins had attacked Point Pleasant—at the mouth of Kanawha. Our town was instantly in commotion, and in a very short time a large force of armed men left for that place. The steamboat *Victor* with three howitzers on board, and some soldiers under command of Capt. Baggs, soon hove in sight of the Point. The land forces with musketry and a rifled cannon arrived opposite the town about the same time. The 'Trumbull Guards," under command of Lieutenants Gilman and Freer, were amongst the first to cross the river, and conducted themselves like veterans. Their prompt action and bravery is worthy of the highest praise. The soldiers from the Hospital also turned out to the number of 100, armed and ready for fight, though many were really very ill.

THE BATTLE OF HURRICANE BRIDGE, MARCH 28, 1863

The rebels up to that time had set on fire a large quantity of corn and some buildings containing commissary stores. One company of the 13th Va. had taken refuge in the Court House and were successfully defending themselves against five times their number. On seeing the reinforcements the guerrillas hastily skedaddled, leaving four or five dead, and taking several wounded with them, stealing at the same time about 25 mules belonging to the United States. Our men on searching the town, found thirteen of the rebels concealed in private houses all of whom were safely lodged in our jail. Among them are one Captain and three Lieutenants. On their way to this place on board the Victor, one of the scamps became very insolent to Capt. Ford, who by the way resides in the Point—and of course not in a humor to submit to anything of the kind. The captain very soon taught him a lesson he will remember. On the whole the rebels were completely defeated. Captain Carter of the 13th and his men fought like tigers. – They lost one man killed and three wounded. The rebel loss was 5 killed, several wounded and 13 taken prisoners. The cowardly knaves shot Col. Wagoner, a man nearly 80 years of age, then on his way home, and robbed him of his horse.

He was one of the few staunch Union men in that quarter and deserved a better fate. They fired on defenseless women and children crossing the river in skiffs and in every way showed themselves brutal, cowardly assassins, ready to waylay and murder, merely for plunder. Up to the hour of writing we are unable to say whether they have got safely across Kanawha, or whether General Scammon, has been able to gobble them up. The main body of the Union forces are concentrated about Gauley. We have hopes that General Scammon may be able to checkmate the scoundrel Jenkins and bag the whole crew. – So long as he is suffered to run at large West Virginia must suffer, from his raids, and the sooner a cavalry force is provided to cope with him, the better for the Union cause. Since the above was in type the steamboat B.C. Levi has arrived from Charleston with a detachment of the 23rd O.V. Capt. Regnier reports the rebels in sight near Maupin's landing. – He had a full view of their camp. – They fired several shots at the *Levi*, but all fell short or passed over. The sight of a number of bales of hay on board used as breast works, for the 23d induced them to keep out of range. Capt. Ford of the Victor reports 21 rebels found dead in and near the Point, and two more prisoners captured. – Thus the robbers have paid pretty well for their plunder. The federal loss, 2 killed three wounded. If proper efforts be made the whole gang may yet be captured. Later. – The rebels admit to a loss of 70 killed, wounded and missing."[18]

Another editorial appeared in the *Gallipolis Journal* on the same date:

> The rebels have again made their appearance in the Kanawha Valley in considerable force. On last Saturday a detachment of Jenkins' cavalry, under command of that renowned freebooter and robber in person, attacked a detachment of the 13th Virginia, in camp at Hurricane Bridge, and were whipped out, but the force was too small to follow up the marauders. On Sunday they fired into our government steamboats *Victor No. 2* and *Gen'l Meigs*, on their way down the Kanawha. The attack was quite unexpected on part of the officers of the boats, and for about one and a half miles they were obliged to run the gauntlet of an incessant fire from behind every tree, stump, fence, or shield of any kind. The boats were entirely unprotected, and unarmed, and the numerous bullet holes to the number of 200 in each, show the fierceness of the attack.
>
> The pilots on board of each deserve the highest praise of the noble manner in which they stood to the wheel. The pilot-house of the *Gen'l Meigs* is completely riddled with balls. We noticed one spoke of the wheel nearly severed by a ball, and from its position the handle must have been held by the pilot at the very instant. His name is Edward Johnson. A braver fellow than he is does not live, nor a better Union man. Capt. Summers, in command of the *Meigs*, stood to his post like a man, and by his coolness and daring provided himself the 'right man in the right place.' On board the *Meigs* no one was injured. The *Victor* was the first boat to pass through the fire. Capt. Ford, though his boat was

crowded with passengers, evinced the coolest daring, firmness, and courage possible for any man under like circumstances. The pilots, Harry Bays and Stape Wright, never flinched for an instant, but without any protection, regardless of the crashing of the Minnie [sic - minié] balls through every portion of the boat, and especially the pilot house, brought off the boat in safety, with the loss of one man killed, Frank Stote, teamster, and one mortally wounded.—How scores escaped being killed or wounded on this boat, is a mystery.

Drawn into ambuscade without the slightest warning, and without any protection other than the frail siding of the cabin, crowded as it was with women and children, their escape was truly miraculous. Too much praise cannot be awarded the pilots and officers of these boats, and we trust their courageous conduct will receive proper encouragement from Head-quarters.— They deserve honorable mention in all papers in this District. Such true bravery is too rare in this day to go unrewarded. Let us see if the commanding officers appreciate it. We are sure the passengers on board did.[19]

The March 30, 1863, attack on Point Pleasant left the locals debating the causes and various outcomes for weeks, as well as continuing to throw rebuttals at Captain John Carter, who commanded the Union troops there. The following opinion appeared in the *Gallipolis Journal* on April 15, 1863:

The little fight at Point Pleasant has occasioned more talk and discussion in these parts than any battle fought during the war. Whole pages of newspapers have been taken up in its discussion, or rather in the discussion as to who was the most deserving of praise. Each disputant has his favorite and sticks as tenacious to him as a hungry bulldog would to his bone. The Capt. Commanding Post has rushed into the midst of the scene and claims for his brave boys the exclusive victory. They did well, nobly, and will ever stand honored for their bravery in the hearts of a grateful [sic] people. The captain in his eagerness to set us right in our statement, in his letter published in our columns last

JENKINS ATTACKS AT POINT PLEASANT MARCH 30, 1863

week, exhibited the animal pretty largely. His efforts to detract from others the credit and praise due them, is ungrateful to say the least.

His letter we knew to be untrue in many particulars and debated in our mind the propriety of its publication but believing it due to the soldiers and citizens here who went to the rescue of our sister town, that they should know the manner in which their promptness of action, and the result of that promptness, was viewed by those they rescued, we gave it to the public. We need call attention to but one or two points in Capt. Carter's letter to show up the inconsistency of the whole of it. We quote from his letter: 'There was shown in the streets before we entered the Court house.' If he will take his own town paper he will find it there stated, if not in the exact words, that which amounts to the same, that immediately upon the alarm Capt. Carter ran to the camp and collected his men into the Court-house, which arrangement had been previously agreed upon, and there maintained the contest. Again, we quote from his letter: 'There were enough soldiers in Pt. Pleasant to whip the rebels; which they did, before help arrived.'

If such be the case, we cannot understand why Capt. Carter was beleaguered in the Court-house. If the rebels were whipped before reinforcements arrived from Gallipolis, why did he not have his company out of the Court-house picking up the rebel stragglers? How did it happen that they were mostly captured by the Trumbull Guards, soldiers from the Gallipolis Hospital, and the armed citizens of Ohio? Again we quote from his letter: 'I award great credit to the Trumbull Guards, and citizens, who did cross to our assistance, notwithstanding the enemy had retreated.' And what caused the enemy to retreat? They had possession of the town and the Federal soldiers under Capt. Carter were beleaguered in the Court-house. Does anyone besides Capt. Carter say that under such circumstances the rebels retreated because they were whipped by the Federal soldiers then in Pt. Pleasant, and the retreat was not made in consequence of the arrival of the reinforcements from Ohio? Again we quote: 'The first act which the men in command of the artillery did was to range their course for the Court-house and was prevented from firing upon us by the earnest entreaty of some of the citizens of Pt. Pleasant who happened to be on that side of the river.' The artillerymen as well as citizens tell us this statement is unqualifiedly false. But we have called attention to enough of the captain's publication to show the absurdity of it.[20]

Mason County Court House, 1857. Courtesy Courthousehistory.com

JENKINS ATTACKS AT POINT PLEASANT MARCH 30, 1863

News of the battle at Point Pleasant, along with the obligatory rumor mills, quickly spread across the Kanawha Valley. Captain John Valley Young and Company G was stationed at Coalsmouth, twelve miles away from Hurricane Bridge at the time of the March 28, 1863 battle. Company G served at several other outposts throughout the Kanawha Valley throughout the war. Most of the men in Company G were usually close to their home area in the valley, but often in reality, they may as well have been a thousand miles away, as they were typically unable to get leave to return home and had to write letters instead.

When news of the fighting at Hurricane Bridge and Point Pleasant reached Coalsmouth a few days later, Young wrote to Captain Edgar Blundon, who commanded Company F of the 8th West Virginia Infantry; that regiment was formerly stationed in the Kanawha Valley, where most of its men were from, but had recently been relocated to Buckhannon, West Virginia. Blundon was engaged to Young's twenty-year-old daughter, Sarah Francis Young, a.k.a. "Sallie." Young quite overestimated Jenkins' numbers but was clearly pleased to learn of his withdrawal from Hurricane and defeat at Point Pleasant. The captains communicated regularly throughout the war, and Young wrote the following on April 5, 1863:

> Dear Captain, As I have an opportunity to send a letter direct by Mr. Walls, I will try and give you some of the news of the valley…Old Jenkins made his raid into the valley and has gotten out again, but he never called on me but went around me and attacked the Hurricane Bridge, got whipped there, then marched to the Point, where Captain [John] Carter and his brave lads flogged him again. Then, he turned his course up the river, crossed at ten-mile, and struck a bee line for Mud [River], but Captain [George] Rucker, with his Home Guards, pitched into him and bushwhacked him to Mud River. The thief came in with eight hundred, but I don't think he got out with three hundred. He stole about one hundred head of horses and a great deal of other property, and it all might well have been saved.
>
> Jenkins might have been caught but escaped. Colonel Brown wanted to go but was unable. So as it is, he is out and gone. The whole country is full of squads of robbers. Three companies

maintained their ground against six hundred. The firing commenced at 6 AM and lasted until half past eleven. (I mean at the Hurricane Bridge). The whole country is in a state of excitement...They say that he [Jenkins] has about eight hundred men, and when they rest he intends another attack on the 13th [West Virginia] at this place and the Hurricane Bridge...I have my company and Company I here, in all about one hundred men, but if old Jenk does come I think he will have a good time of it.[21]

Following the battles at Hurricane Bridge and Point Pleasant, Companies E and F were sent to Mud Bridge in Cabell County in late April, where they quickly dug up earth works around the Union Baptist Church. The remaining companies A, B, D and H spent the next month at Hurricane Bridge improving and strengthening their earthen fort; Company G was at Coalsmouth, and C was sent to Winfield.[22]

The weather at Hurricane Bridge was unpredictable to say the least during March-April 1863. Dr. Samuel G. Shaw wrote to his daughters on March 30, 1863, that it was "spring like" only to experience "one of the fiercest snowstorms of the season" the next day. On April 1, 1863, he noted "The temperature is that of January rather than April." The 23rd Ohio Infantry regiment arrived to strengthen the Union garrison at Hurricane Bridge on April 3, 1863. Captain James W. Johnson took advantage of the increased troop strength and set his men about the task of enlarging and strengthening their earthen fortifications. Dr. Shaw recalled a heavy rainstorm at Hurricane Bridge on the night of April 6, 1863, when he wrote,

> Today they have commenced enlarging and strengthening the fortifications, they have had eight yokes of oxen drawing up very large logs for this purpose. At the time of the fight the fort was not completed, it has been much improved since and will be still further improved. I have not been able to see the necessity or expediency of keeping a regiment at this place.[23]

Chapter Seven References

1. 13th West Virginia Field History, Part 1; Civil War Recollections of George Rucker, Co. E, 13th West Virginia Infantry, Letter of September 19, 1862, Rucker Family Papers, MS-94.45, WV State Archives; OR, Series 1, Vol. 25, Part 1, 76-77.

2. 13th West Virginia Field History, Part 1; Conner, 7-8; Wintz, Vol. 1, 88; "The services of Capt. Fred. Ford, in the Late War." *Weekly Register*, December 3, 1868. Vol. 7, (20), *Gallipolis Journal*, April 2, 1863, Vol. 28(19), 2. Capt. Frederick Ford Navy Pension File, Feb. 15, 1882. Letter by Major B.R. Cowen, Army Paymaster, to Brig. Gen. B.F. Scammon, June 5, 1863, Claim No. 7945, Microfilm T288, Roll 157, National Archives. (Hereafter Frederick Ford Pension file) Captain Frederick Ford was a strong Unionist and emancipation supporter; he was later sued by James Ruffner in Kanawha County Court for transporting a runaway slave valued at $1,500.00 on May 13, 1862. The case was heard in Kanawha County Court on January 6, 1883, and Ruffner won the case.

3. Conner, 7-8.

4. *Gallipolis Journal*, April 9, 1863, Vol. 28(22), 2.

5. Ibid., *Gallipolis Journal*, April 2, 1863, Vol. 28(19), 2.

6. 13th West Virginia Field History, Part 1; Sedinger Diary, 10; Sedinger Wartime Reminiscences, 55-78.

7. Ibid.

8. Miller, Richard F. (Ed.). *States at War: A Reference Guide to Ohio in the Civil War*. Vol. 5. (Lebanon, New Hampshire: University Press of England, 2015), 401; *Tribune Chronicle*, Gallipolis Ohio, April 12, 2015, online: http: www.//Tribtoday.com; Comstock, Jim. Hardesty's Atlas of West Virginia Counties: Mason, Pleasants, Lewis & Roane. (Richwood, WV: Self-published 1973), 27. (Hereafter Comstock).

9. OR Series 1, Vol. 25, Part 1, 75; Sedinger Wartime Reminiscences, 55-78.

10. CSR, RG94, M324, Roll 83, National Archives.

11. Ibid.

12. Sedinger, 75-56; CSR, RG 94, M324, Roll 85, National Archives; Comstock, 27-28.

13. Comstock, 27.

14. OR, Series 1, Vol. 19, 1083; OR, Series 1, Vol. 25, Part 1, 75-76; 13th WV Field History, Part 1; 13th West Virginia Field History, Part 1. WV State Archives; CSR, Union Regiments, 13th West Virginia, RG94, M508, Roll 206, National Archives; WV AG, Union Regiments, 13th West Virginia, AR 382, Box 20, WV State Archives; CSR, RG94, M324, Roll 85, National Archives. Lieutenant William N. Hawkins was commissioned on September 12, 1862, and served in Company E. He served until the end of the war, and he later took command of the company when the captain was wounded on March 1, 1865.
15. Sedinger Diary, 10.
16. OR Series 1, Vol. 25, Part 1, 76.
17. *Weekly Register,* Vol. 2(5), April 16, 1863, 2.
18. *Gallipolis Journal,* April 2, 1863. www.galliagenealogy.com.
19. Ibid.
20. Ibid.
21. J.V. Young Letters, April 5, 1863.
22. 13th WV Field History, Part 1.
23. Dr. Shaw Letters, April 6, 1863.

CHAPTER EIGHT

AFTER THE BATTLE AT HURRICANE BRIDGE

Shortly after the battle at Hurricane Bridge, West Virginia was formally admitted into the Union as a new state on June 20, 1863. While the 13th West Virginia troops later fought in much larger battles of the war, many veterans correctly viewed their service in the Kanawha Valley as playing a key role in helping the Reformed Government of Virginia obtain statehood. However, the outpost at Hurricane Bridge quickly became a very unpopular duty station among the Union soldiers in the area. Essentially a remote, isolated fort, it was blatantly exposed to attack from many directions, and there were persistent problems with disease plaguing the garrisons there throughout the war.

Captain James Johnson, commanding the outpost, did not post pickets (sentries) guarding access to the garrison camp following the March 28, 1863, battle. Apparently, the Union troops returned to the dull routine of camp duties, convinced the immediate threat was resolved. According to Dr. Samuel G. Shaw, who wrote, "There is no security here outside the camp. I spend a part of the day generally in camp. Yesterday we had general inspection and dress parade, the first since I have been here." Shaw told his daughters in a letter of April 7, 1863, things were

THE BATTLE OF HURRICANE BRIDGE, MARCH 28, 1863

"All quiet on the Hurricane as they say of the Potomac. We have a cool, chilly and disagreeable morning, a regular northern spell of weather."

Private David Burrows, Company F, 13th West Virginia Volunteer Infantry, was one of the soldiers who later became intimately acquainted with the hardships of garrisoning that isolated outpost after the March 28, 1863, battle. Once Federal officers learned of the attack, Company F was ordered to Hurricane Bridge from Point Pleasant but did not arrive in time to participate in the battle. Typical of soldiers in the field, Burrows wasted no time expressing to his family his thoughts about what occurred there. He opined that one of the reasons Jenkins had been able to easily attack the post was because Union officials were not aware of his approach, due to the remote location, until March 28, 1863. On April 4, 1863, Company F was still at Hurricane Bridge, and Burrows groused, "I don't know when we will get away from here. Some of the boys had a fight up here, but we did not get in on it…we have been on one big scout since we have been up here."

Dr. Samuel G. Shaw was similarly convinced "This place seems to be cut off from all the rest of creation at present" during his time at Hurricane Bridge. Corporal John Hess of Company D wrote to his wife Samantha on April 10, 1863, "I set on my bed which is straw with a sad heart" and expressed intense homesickness, "I can't bear it" from the isolation at the lonely outpost. They were also having trouble getting enough food, as Hess told his wife, "Tell Leon to fit up the regiment with corn shocks." Soon, the boredom of camp led to mischief, as Hess also noted " the boys is so bad that I can't write a lot…I expect that you can't read it – I can't rite it makes me feel bad…" Rations were mostly poor beef and hardtack crackers, even in the summer, as they rarely had time to cook it while out on patrol. Their pay was also slow making it to camp, as Hess griped to his wife, "I had to eat raw meat and crackers for breakfast all the time I was glad to get it…I cant get no money we will get 4 months pay next week."

Another incident occurred on April 10, 1863, which further characterizes the personal nature of the Civil War in West Virginia. Colonel Milton Ferguson, who commanded the 8th Virginia Cavalry, had returned to his home in Wayne County for a brief visit. On that date he and Captain Hurston Spurlock, who was also from Wayne County, took nine of their men and arrested Hiram Bloss, a known Union supporter.

AFTER THE BATTLE AT HURRICANE BRIDGE

He was sent to prison at Richmond and described as "loathsome and filthy." His health suffered so severely that after the war he filed a lawsuit against Ferguson and the other captors for $10,000.00 damages. Spurlock was later accused of murdering a Union officer who had surrendered in 1864.[1]

Captain David Love, 2nd West Virginia Cavalry, went on an expedition from Camp Piatt through Logan and Cabell Counties during April 3-6, 1863, and his battalion was engaged in a small skirmish with Confederate cavalry under General Jenkins at Mud River on April 6, 1863; he found also that several companies of cavalry belonging to Colonel James Sweeney's battalion were with Jenkins. Captain Love wrote,

> ...I learned that he had marched in the direction of Mud River, leaving the Guyandotte road. Not having a guide, I had to follow his trail through one of the wildest sections of country in Western Virginia. About 3 o'clock I struck the Mud River road and traveled up it 1 mile to where the trail again left the road, and crossed the river and ascended a very steep and rough hill, covered by thick woods. When the advance was about half way down the hill, on the opposite side, it came upon the enemy in a very deep ravine, into which it was almost impossible to force the horses. After a sharp skirmish, we drove them from their position, when a very exciting and dangerous chase ensued, the enemy scattering in every direction. During the engagement the enemy lost 1 man killed and 15 prisoners, 15 horses, and 50 stand of arms, which we destroyed. After resting an hour, I started for Hurricane Bridge, arriving there at 8 o'clock, and remained there during the night.

However, Dr. Samuel Shaw wrote that the 2nd West Virginia Cavalry had brought in thirty-three prisoners, six or seven of whom were seriously ill, and most were barefoot.[2]

On April 15, 1863 Colonel William Brown petitioned the U.S. War Department to have Captain James W. Johnson transferred to the 3rd United States Colored Troops; Johnson had tendered his resignation on May 15, 1863, and requested transfer into the 3rd U.S. Colored Troops, which was approved on July 25, 1863. Colonel Brown wrote that he regretted having to "part with so valuable an officer and high minded gentleman," noting also that Captain Johnson was leaving to accept a higher position than he presently held. However, when Johnson transferred on July 25, 1863, he became a 1st Lieutenant, one pay grade lower than what he was in the 13th West Virginia. The United States government authorized forming regiments comprised of African American men in 1862. In May 1863, under the auspices of the War Department, the Bureau of Colored Troops was authorized, with the contingency that white officers must command the regiments. The 3rd U.S. Colored Regiment was organized at Philadelphia, Pennsylvania, on August 3 and served in the 10th Corps at South Carolina and Florida.[3]

The 13th West Virginia Infantry lost only four men killed in battle during 1863, all at Hurricane Bridge. They spent the remainder of 1863 in the Kanawha Valley region, although later fought in much larger engagements, such as at Fayetteville in May 1863 and the capture of Brigadier General John Hunt Morgan's Confederate cavalry brigade at Buffington Island in July 1863. They later served under future United States President Rutherford B. Hayes, who commanded their brigade in the Shenandoah Valley Campaign in 1864, where they fought at Lynchburg, Lexington, and witnessed the Virginia Military Institute, Major General Thomas "Stonewall" Jackson's alma mater, burned to the ground, and were also engaged in major battles at Kernstown, Berryville, Winchester (Opequon), Fisher's Hill and Cedar Creek. The March 28, 1863, Battle at Hurricane Bridge was certainly a small factor in context of the larger strategic outcome of the Civil War but was highly significant to the men who fought there and to the civilians residing in the area.

Many of the veterans later recalled "seeing the Elephant" first at Hurricane Bridge in Putnam County. This meant to experience combat for the first time in Civil War parlance. For the Union soldiers, it was also a test of their mettle and commitment, and for many who were fighting with typhoid and other illnesses, it was no small feat. This was also their first battle working as a cohesive fighting unit, as heretofore, the 13th West Virginia had mainly operated as solo companies on patrols or garrisoning outposts across the region. The battle at Hurricane Bridge was important as "Globed sighted rifles" were used, enabling the sharpshooters to better zero in on their targets at longer distances, which later became a standard practice in military tactics. The engagement is inscribed as a battle honor on their 1865 Regimental Battle Flag, as a final testament to its importance to the men who fought there. Colonel William Brown also made a list of the "principal battles" the regiment was involved with and included Hurricane Bridge along with major battles they participated in during the 1864 Shenandoah Valley Campaign. If the battle at Hurricane Bridge was not significant, the veterans would have omitted it. The small village of Hurricane, on the other hand, truly became forever associated with the Civil War in West Virginia.[4]

The 8th and 16th Virginia Cavalry Regiments continued to serve in the Kanawha Valley throughout 1863, and then went on to fight in the Shenandoah Valley Campaign in 1864 and were also at the battle of Monocacy on July 9, 1864. The 16th Virginia Cavalry also participated in the Gettysburg Campaign in June-July 1863. Sergeant James D. Sedinger participated in virtually every battle in the Kanawha Valley and was elected as 2nd Lieutenant by his comrades on February 8, 1864. He served with Jenkins in the Gettysburg campaign and was also in the 1864 Shenandoah Valley Campaign with Jenkins. He was captured at Fishers Hill, Virginia on September 22, 1864, and remained a prisoner of war until the end of the war.[5]

Should Jenkins have fought at Hurricane Bridge?

Several historians have questioned General Albert Jenkins' decision to fight at Hurricane Bridge. He was not aware of the Federal presence there until he arrived at Hamlin (modern Lincoln County) on March 27, 1863, when a citizen informed him of their general strength and location. One writer stated, "Jenkins obviously made a colossal blunder in making a threat without showing his force to back it up. Otherwise, his plan might have succeeded. Knowing he had the Federals outnumbered four to one, he could have indeed surrounded them, and made a frontal assault, and captured the position. But he didn't want it – he just wanted the Yankees out of his way. Perhaps Captain James Johnson thought Jenkins was bluffing, but if he had seen the number of Confederates he was facing, he might have given a different answer to Major Nounnan. There is no indication he had any idea of enemy strength until the skirmish started." That author also opined Jenkins never intended to capture the Union fort, arguing this was because Jenkins' men were dismounted, which was usually a defensive, rather than offensive, tactic for cavalrymen in the Civil War era. Another notion commonly suggested as to why Jenkins did not attack in a massed infantry column and overwhelm the Union position is because they lacked infantry training, which was not the case. Jenkins' battalion spent the winter months drilling as infantry, although as noted earlier in Chapter Six, many of his officers were also newly commissioned and inexperienced with infantry tactics in actual combat. Several of the eleven companies in Jenkins' battalion were formerly infantry units in 1861. In particular, Company E, 8th Virginia Cavalry, were formerly known as the Fairview Rifles and fought with the 167th Regiment, Virginia Militia, at the battle of Barboursville on July 14, 1861. Colonel Milton J. Ferguson, who commanded the 8th Virginia Cavalry, had initially raised the company. He wrote in a post-war recollection, "My company the Fairview Rifles was taken in the State Service, but when we were turned over to the Confederate States was put into the Cavalry in the 8th Va…I was made Cap. of Co. K, 8th Va. Cav. known as the Big Sandy Rangers."

Yet another commonly suggested reason the Confederates did not do a frontal assault on the fort was a lack of infantry weapons; Private Thomas P. Copenshaver of the 8th Virginia Cavalry indicated several troopers from that regiment were carrying double-barreled shotguns earlier in the war, "until supplied from Federal troops." The latter implies they later acquired more effective weapons confiscated from Federals, likely cavalry carbines. However, Jenkins also received 600 Richmond Muskets prior to beginning his raid into western Virginia, and he also had sharpshooters armed with Whitworth Globed rifles, then considered the premier "sniper" rifle of the era. Hence, it is unlikely Jenkins did not attempt to capture the Union fort due to lack of infantry training or lacking infantry weapons.[6]

Another common assumption about the battle at Hurricane Bridge is that Jenkins allowed the battle to continue for five hours hoping that the Federals would "see the hopelessness of the situation and surrender." At least one researcher also argued it continued so long because the Federal commander, Captain James Johnson, realized that his men suffered "little damage" from the Confederate cross fire, and simply kept fighting.

Much of this scenario was discussed in Chapter Six, but it is not accurate to state that Captain Johnson was unaffected by the long range rifle fire; he blatantly stated in his official report, "…the enemy appeared in force and poured a furious fire upon us simultaneously on three sides, from as many different hills, owing to the high elevation of which, and the unfinished condition of our works, exposed our men to a galling cross fire…The enemy's sharpshooters posted on the adjacent heights and armed with globe sighted Rifles were constantly endeavoring to pick off officers and men…"

Federal casualties at Hurricane Bridge were four killed, one mortally wounded and three wounded, including one "severely wounded" by gunshot through both thighs, and one with a minor head wound. The regimental adjutant was killed by multiple gunshot wounds, which is attributable to his post near Captain Johnson, a few yards behind the earth works in an exposed position. So, it is easy to see there was more than "little damage" done to Union troops at Hurricane Bridge.

If one considers the heavy cloud of gray smoke covering the area where the Union fort was located, use of earth works and the general distance between opposing forces, it is not surprising that nearly five hours lapsed during the battle at Hurricane Bridge. Poor visibility alone required both Union and Confederate soldiers to take more time and make deliberate, well aimed shots through the haze, and considering it took an experienced soldier fifteen to twenty seconds to reload the muzzle loading percussion weapons used in that era, a four to five hour time lapse seems almost a logical outcome.[7]

Summarily, the answer to the question of whether or not Jenkins should have fought at Hurricane Bridge seems clear. Once he discovered the Union garrison blocking his route to and from Point Pleasant, it became imperative that he attack. It was first of all consistent with his overall mission objectives, and more importantly, he knew that if he did not deal with the Union garrison then, they would have plenty of time to reinforce before he returned encumbered with heavy wagon trains and possibly a herd of beef cattle. In that sense, an attack was necessary. However, as is typical in warfare, Jenkins' plans did not go accordingly, and he failed to capture the garrison, and ultimately withdrew.

Jenkins lost more than seventy men killed and wounded at Point Pleasant, and several were captured; not to mention he failed to obtain the herd of beef cattle. Perhaps the outcome would have been different were his troopers mounted on horses versus going on foot. Some writers have posited that the battle at Hurricane Bridge was a "dismal failure" for Jenkins and never should have happened in the first place. Yet, Jenkins should not be faulted for giving battle under those circumstances. It certainly had the desired effect of making his presence known in the Kanawha Valley once more, and it clearly caused Brigadier General E.P. Scammon to become anxious and apprehensive regarding moving his troops about the valley afterward, and in the chivalrous military culture of the era, Jenkins also knew that he would have been questioned by his superiors for not making at least a demonstration when he encountered the Union troops.

The issue of overall success in Jenkins' raid is not up for debate, however. During his attacks at Hurricane, Point Pleasant, Chapmanville and smaller skirmishes on the return march south, through Wayne and Cabell Counties, he lost more than twenty percent of his troops killed, wounded, captured or taken with illness. That is a steep price to pay with minimal results. On April 15, 1863, General Jones telegraphed Jenkins asking how many men he had for immediate service.

Jenkins replied "I can furnish about 1,000 men for immediate service, but not more than 300 of them are armed. The men who went with me on my late expedition have not returned yet, and they would not be fit for service if they were here." In the end, although each of Jenkins' cavalry regiments involved at Hurricane Bridge went on to establish impressive combat records, the raid of March 1863 was in fact a "dismal failure" for the Confederates, and a small, but logistically and tactically important victory for the largely inexperienced Union troops, who withstood a withering fire, holding their position "with the firmness of Veterans."[8]

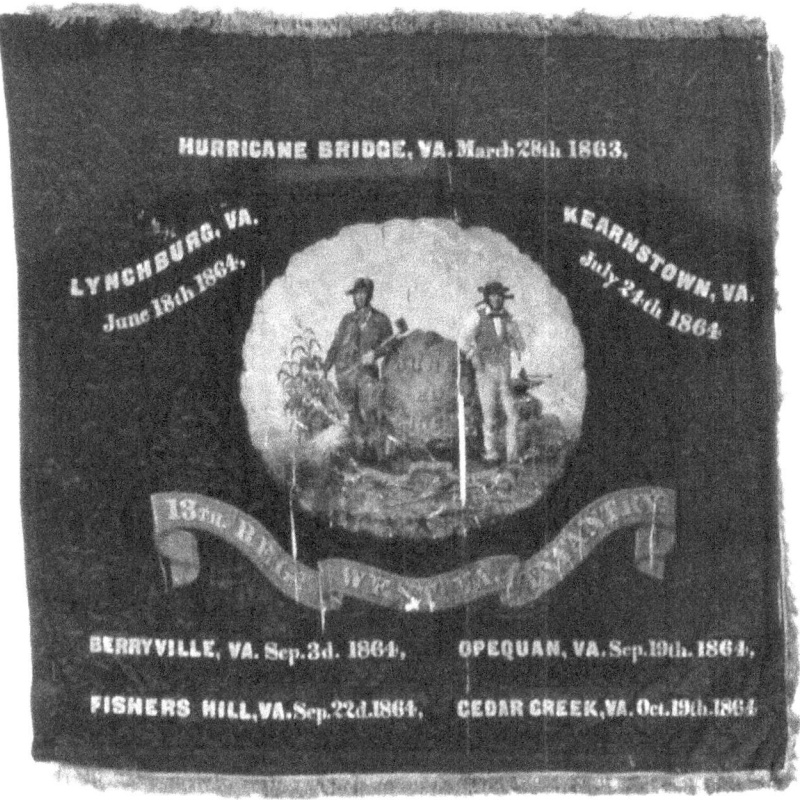

Regimental flag of the 13th West Virginia Volunteer Infantry. West Virginia State Museum.

Chapter Eight References

1. Dr. Shaw Letters, April 4, 6 & 7, 1863; Hess Letters, April 10 and June 7, 1863; Thompson, Life of Colonel Milton Ferguson, 73; Burns, Edward E. *Standard Encyclopedia of Procedure.* Vol. 9, (Los Angeles, CA: L.D. Powell Co., 1914), 497.
2. OR Series 1, Vol. 25, Part 1, 70-80; Dr. Shaw Letters, April 6, 1863.
3. CSR, 13th West Virginia, RG 94, M508, Roll 207, National Archives. See also: Dobak, William. *Freedom by the Sword: The U.S. Colored Troops 1862-1867.* (Carlisle, PA: U.S. Army Military History Center, Published by Library of Congress, 2011).
4. Roush, 12-13, 26-29. Call No. 973.781 R863, WV State Archives; CSR, 13th West Virginia, RG 94, M508, Roll 207, National Archives; WV AG Papers, AR 382, Box 20, 13th West Virginia Infantry, Folder 1, WV State Archives; 13th West Virginia Field History, Part 2, WV State Archives.
5. Miller, O.R. Skirmish at Hurricane Bridge; Dickinson, 8th Va. Cavalry, p. 44-56; Dickinson *16th Virginia Cavalry,* 20-32; CSR, RG 94, 8th Virginia Cavalry, M324, Roll 146, National Archives; OR, Series 1, Vol. 25, Part 2, 722-723.
6. Miller, O.R. Skirmish at Hurricane Bridge; Conner, 6; Copenshaver, Thomas P. Civil War Letters, 1-2; *Wheeling Intelligencer,* February 21, 1863.
7. Hurricane Centennial Committee, 4-6; 13th West Virginia Field History, Part 1, Appendix A; OR, Series 1, Vol. 19, 1083; Hurricane Centennial, 4-7.
8. Miller, O.R. Skirmish at Hurricane Bridge; Dickinson, 8th Va. Cavalry, 44-56; Dickinson *16th Virginia Cavalry,* 31-32; OR, Series 1, Vol. 25, Part 2, 722-723; Conner, 6-8; Brownlee, K. 13th WV, 12-15.

Epilogue

SECOND BATTLE AT HURRICANE BRIDGE

There were other Federal regiments who served at Hurricane Bridge later in the war, including the 141st Ohio National Guard, but for the majority of 1863, it was the 13th West Virginia Volunteer Infantry. Captain John Valley Young's Company G was stationed at Coalsmouth eleven miles away at the time of the March 28, 1863, battle, and was stationed at several similar outposts throughout the Kanawha Valley throughout the war. They were quite mobile, and although close to home, often in reality, they may as well have been a thousand miles away, as they were typically unable to get furloughs to return home. Captain Young and his Company G were ordered to garrison Hurricane Bridge later, in early December 1863.

While muster roll data is incomplete for the company during this period, it is estimated Young had approximately ninety to one hundred men near the end of November. There, the company manned picket posts, sent patrols into the nearby village of Hurricane and surrounding areas, and also arrested several Confederate citizens. After receiving orders from the War Department in November that the company was being assigned to the 11th West Virginia, Colonel William Brown promptly recalled about forty-seven of Young's men to Barboursville on December 3, 1863, and shrewdly ordered them to fill in ranks of the other companies in his own regiment. Brown argued it was his regiment's presence in the Kanawha Valley area that initially attracted those men to enlist in the first place, and he was therefore entitled to them. This infuriated Young, who had recruited those men after his initial affiliation with the 13th West Virginia in August 1862.

Young was already agitated from a series of ongoing quarrels with army paymasters and supply problems (it was nearly December 1862 before he and his company were able to draw complete uniforms from quartermasters), and he did not look forward to spending time at the remote outpost with a company operating at half strength. Young wrote to his wife on December 3, 1863, stating he did not think there was imminent danger from Confederates; however, when he wrote to Colonel Brown on December 11, 1863, he had dramatically changed his mind on the latter.[1]

Young was also still stinging from Colonel Brown's move to re-distribute his troops into other companies when he received a new dispatch from Union headquarters in Charleston on December 10, 1864, ordering him to send a lieutenant and twenty-six men to Coalsmouth, which would leave him with about fifteen men at Hurricane Bridge; the officer wrote that the Assistant Adjutant General had advised him,

> If you think it necessary to send a Lieut and 25 men of Capt Young's Company to Coals Mouth, do so. From representations made to me by Mr. Benedict I do think it is necessary: and therefore, require that you will comply with the Adjutant Generals Order, and notify your Regimental Commander thereof immediately.

The Mr. Benedict referred to in the letter was likely Samuel Benedict of Coalsmouth, a wealthy and influential attorney and strong Unionist. He was also one of the representatives who helped draft the new state constitution in 1861, as well as the father-in-law of John S. Cunningham, the adjutant of the 13th West Virginia Infantry. Benedict sent several letters to both the Governor and the state Adjutant General during the war, usually complaining (rightfully so) that Coalsmouth was not secure from Confederate raids. In November 1863, he had sent another letter requesting arms for their Citizen Patrol. His son-in-law was Captain John S. Cunningham, who had recently replaced 1st Lieutenant Emory Bridgeman, who was killed in action at Hurricane Bridge on March 28, 1863, as Adjutant of the 13th West Virginia. Cunningham was a popular officer and had won Colonel William Brown's favor.

Young was incensed, and wrote to Colonel Brown on December 11, 1863, from Hurricane Bridge,

AFTER THE BATTLE AT HURRICANE BRIDGE

I have the honor wherein to enclose copies of orders received today, and you can imagine my surprise on their receipt, to think that I have been placed here on this rebel thoroughfare with my Company, where we are in danger day & night and then by other representation to have the company divided so as to be sure that some of us may be captured or killed. (It makes me indignant) You know that I never have flinched from duty since I have been in the service but this trys my patience and I think the request is beyond precedent. I suppose that you have not learned that Provost Marshall has arrested a great number of rebel women and men in Putnam, this week, and taken them to Charleston and they are now in the Guard House, and the rebels here say they will have revenge in a few days. I understand today, that they are threatening that they will have Union women taken as hostages and that in a few days. I learned yesterday that notorious horse thief Wake Dudding is in, I had Sergt McDaniel and 12 men after him last night, and but for this order would have at him tonight.[2]

Needless to say, Young was not happy to comply with orders to further divide his company. His previous assumption that the area was free of Confederates on December 3, 1863, quickly proved to be inaccurate; Soon there was another attack on the Union garrison at Hurricane Bridge with only about forty-two men present in Company G to defend the post. Ironically, that was the same group of men Young originally recruited in 1861. On the bitter cold afternoon of Sunday, December 13, 1863, Young was alerted by his pickets that a large force of enemy cavalry was rapidly approaching the post. The Confederates were later identified as some 300-500 men from the 16th Virginia Cavalry, who belonged to Brigadier General Albert Jenkins' cavalry brigade, the same outfit that attacked the outpost with the 8th Virginia Cavalry on March 28, 1863.

Young received a written demand for surrender prior to the assault, which he promptly declined, just as the former garrison commander, Captain James Johnson of the 13th West Virginia, had done nine months previous. Recalling that the majority of the 13th West Virginia were then stationed at nearby Barboursville some thirty miles west, and knowing he was significantly outgunned, the contentious Young decided to fight anyway rather than surrender. This was in many ways likely due to confidence in both his men's fighting tenacity and a great deal of protection afforded by the improved earth works.

The Confederates attacked, and again deployed sharpshooters along the heights as in the previous battle, but they did not then have Whitworth rifles, as those were with Jenkins' troopers in eastern Tennessee at that time. Captain Young's small company fiercely resisted the Confederate attack until just after dark, when he realized that a decision must be made whether or not to evacuate the post. Young later reported, "The enemy left, probably about the same time in great haste…It is doubtful whether they discovered that our force had left." There were no casualties, but in his retreat toward Barboursville, Young found he had two men missing. The Confederates withdrew and likewise moved toward Barboursville, where there was no telegraphic communication with the Union troops' brigade headquarters at Point Pleasant to call for reinforcements if needed, but at least one more regiment, the 5th West Virginia, was in the vicinity.[2]

When Confederates retreated from Hurricane Bridge, Young's company traversed the old James River Turnpike as far as Milton searching for them but found nothing. A few days later, Young received orders to join the Union garrison located at Barboursville, commanded by Lieutenant Colonel James R. Hall of the 13th West Virginia Volunteer Infantry. Hall immediately organized a search party of approximately two hundred infantrymen, including Young's company, and scouted throughout Cabell and Wayne counties looking for Jenkins' Confederates, only this time ran into them. Hall wrote that, "We passed through the country between this and Wayne Court House and found that they were camping in the neighborhood of Wayne Court House. I found it impossible to force them to fight, as they were well mounted and appeared to be only disposed to interrupt us by harassing our advance and rear guards…I would have remained out longer but for the want of rations and the sudden change in and inclemency of the weather, which rendered it impossible for the men to march."[3]

On December 15, 1863, news of the most recent fight at Hurricane Bridge reached Major General B.F. Kelley, who then commanded the Union armies in West Virginia, via Lieutenant Colonel James R. Hall, who was Colonel William Brown's Executive Officer and immediate successor in the 13th West Virginia. Hall telegraphed, "General: Kelley's dispatch just received. The information of the approach of the enemy came from Camp Piatt, Gallipolis, and Barboursville simultaneously. I had no force with which to make any attempt to cut them off. Two gunboats were extemporized-one here, to patrol down the river, and one at Gallipolis, to patrol up. One small party succeeded in crossing during the night and cut the wire near Red House. No other damage has been done. The lines are now up. The enemy attacked a small force at Hurricane Bridge Sunday (13th) afternoon. That night our forces escaped, with 2 missing. The enemy left, probably at about the same time in great haste, going toward Barboursville, taking nothing with them. It is doubtful whether they discovered that our force had left. Our force was only half a company, Under Captain Young, of the Eleventh [West] Virginia Infantry. The enemy's force was about 300. The Thirteenth [West] Virginia is at Barboursville, not under my command. They may intercept the enemy's retreat. It cannot be done from here. I have no telegraphic communication with Barboursville. Colonel Brown is in command there. Boats will commence running again tomorrow, accompanied by sufficient guards."[4]

Thus, as the year 1863 ended at Hurricane Bridge, there would still be more small skirmishes there until the end of the war, but none as intense as those in 1863. There was still an ever-present danger of disease, although the field hospital had been removed earlier that summer. Several men in the 13th West Virginia became severely ill with fever in the damp, cold weather of December 1863, but this did not stop military activities in the region.

Private David Burrows, Company F, 13th West Virginia, was one of the sick, although he managed to recover in time to receive a furlough home to visit with his family during the Christmas holiday. Burrows wrote a poem in his tent during the time he was ill and shared the missive with his family:

> When I am dead my dearest,
> sing no more songs for me
> Plant there no roses at my heard,
> nor shady Cypress tree

THE BATTLE OF HURRICANE BRIDGE, MARCH 28, 1863

Because the green grass above me,
with showers and dew drops wet
And if thou wilt remember,
and if thou wilt forget;

I shall see not the shadows,
I shall not feel the rain
I shall not hear the nightingale singing,
as if in pain[5]

Epilogue References

1. J.V. Young letters, December 3, 1863; WV AG Files, Union Regiments, AR 382, 13th West Virginia, Folders 10 & 11, 13th West Virginia Field History. WV State Archives.
2. OR, Ser. 1, Vol. 29, Part 1, 977; 13th West Virginia Field History, Part 1.
3. OR, Ser. 1, Vol. 51, Part 1, 1139.
4. OR, Series 1, Vol. 30, Part 1, 977-978.
5. Roush, 19.

Appendix A

Order of Battle

Union

13th West Virginia Volunteer Infantry Regiment
Colonel William R. Brown (not present)

Company A – Captain James W. Johnson, Garrison Commander

Company B – Captain Milton Stewart

Company D – Captain Simon Williams

Company H – Captain Taylor W. Hampton

Nativity: Mason, Putnam and Kanawha Counties, West Virginia; Meigs County, Ohio; England, and North Carolina

Strength: 238 Infantry

Weapons: 1861 Springfield Rifles, .58 caliber; 1862 Austrian Lorenz Rifles (Co. A)

Objective: Guard access to the intersection of the James River and Kanawha River Turnpike and Midland Trail, a critical supply line from the Ohio River into the interior of Virginia

Casualties: 3 KIA, 1 mortally wounded, four wounded

Note: This regiment was officially designated as the 13th Virginia Volunteer Infantry until June 20, 1863, when West Virginia attained statehood.

Confederate

Brigadier General Albert G. Jenkins
8th Virginia Cavalry
Colonel James Corns
Companies C, D, E, G, I and K

16th Virginia Cavalry
Colonel Milton J. Ferguson
Major James Nounnan
Companies D, E, G and K

Nativity: Cabell, Wayne and Putnam Counties

Strength: 500-600 Dismounted Cavalry

Weapons: Richmond Muskets, .69 Caliber; 1855 Harper's Ferry Rifled Muskets, .69 caliber; Whitworth Rifles with Globe Sights, .451 caliber

Objective: Mission to Capture Union Supply Depot at Point Pleasant and receive a herd of beef cattle from Confederate sympathizers in Ohio

Casualties: 1, possibly 2 KIA, 2 Wounded, left on field and captured

Weather Conditions: Temperatures estimated 30-40 degrees Celsius; Heavy rains two weeks prior; roads muddy and still frozen in places. Winter was milder than 1862 but still cold and harsh according to newspapers and soldier letters.

Appendix B

13TH WEST VIRGINIA VOLUNTEER INFANTRY COMPANY A MUSTER ROLL, APRIL 10, 1863

Field & Staff			
NAME	RANK	AGE	COMMENTS
James W. Johnson	Captain	24	Senior captain, Garrison Commander
Emory J. Bridgeman	1st Lt.	21	Adjutant, KIA 03/28/1863; multiple GSW
Charles D. Daley	Surgeon	Un-known	Point Pleasant Hospital on 03/28/1863
William R. Crislip	Chaplain	–	Field Hospital during battle

Company A			
NAME	RANK	AGE	COMMENTS
Greenbury Slack	1st Lt.	25	KIA Winchester 09/19/1864
Samuel S. Mathers	2d Lt.	21	Promoted from Private 02/15/1863
George Danner	1st Sgt.	36	
Miletus Grimstead	Sergeant	26	
Thomas Moore	Sergeant	26	
John W. Baxter	Corporal	29	Died of Consumption 08/12/1863
Abraham Chandler	Corporal	19	

THE BATTLE OF HURRICANE BRIDGE, MARCH 28, 1863

William P. Copen	Corporal	28	
Robert H. Davis	Corporal	29	
William M. Davis	Corporal	31	
John W. Ramsey	Corporal	27	
George Stewart	Corporal	33	
James Abbott	Private	44	
Michael Baxter	Private	22	
Benjamin Boggess	Private	18	
Albert Booker	Private	18	
Amos Brown	Private	28	
William Carter	Private	45	
Andrew J. Cobb	Private	30	
Francis M. Cobb	Private	22	
William A. Cobb	Private	28	
William P. Compton	Private	43	
Andrew J. Davis	Private	23	
John H. Edens	Private	35	
Martin Van Buren Edens	Private	28	
Arron V. Facemiers	Private	21	also spelled Facemyer
Christopher F. Frame	Private	21	Died of brain fever Winfield 11/29/1862
Richard George	Private	30	
William H. George	Private	20	
William M. Glover	Private	23	
John Wesley Good	Private	21	
Robert Gray	Private	24	
William Gray	Private	32	
John Green	Private	38	
Jesse Jobling	Private	23	
Alfred Jones	Private	20	
Samuel Jones	Private	18	Enlisted 03/01/1863 at Hurricane Bridge

William Jones	Private	18	
John C. Kimes	Private	20	
Samuel R. Kimes	Private	20	
George W. King	Private	36	
Theophilus Maher	Private	47	
Samuel McCormick	Private	44	
James A. Means	Private	29	
William A. Means	Private	19	
Alexander H. Miller	Private	18	
John M. Naylor	Private	40	
Elijah F. Newell	Private	41	
Abner Nunley	Private	16	
John Orth	Private	20	
Cornelius Page	Private	54	
Robert J. Pritt	Private	28	
Charles P. Quigley	Private	28	
William W. Riley	Private	21	Pt. Pleasant hospital w/Typhoid May-July 1863
Agrippa Samples	Private	23	
Henry Sands	Private	26	KIA 03/28/1863 Hurricane Bridge
Joseph Scott	Private	48	
David Smith	Private	16	
Andrew S. Snyder	Private	23	
Daniel H. Snodgrass	Private	18	Died of disease Pt. Pleasant 09/02/1863
Nathan Snodgrass	Private	44	Charleston hospital Fever – April-June 1863
James R. Spradling	Private	21	Fever – Pt. Pleasant hospital Dec-Feb 6 1863
Adam Stewart	Private	30	
Ephraim Stewart	Private	22	
John F. Teal	Private	29	
Samuel Teal	Private	24	

John Thomas	Private	51	
James W. Toothman	Private	23	
James Tulley	Private	18	MIA Cedar Creek 10/19/1864; POW to '65
John Tulley	Private	25	
Eli Tulley	Private	18	
George W. Turner	Private	23	
Calvin Vance	Private	20	
Baron De Kalb Wintz	Private	18	
Philip Wintz	Private	18	Enlisted 03/01/1863 at Hurricane Bridge

Company A Statistics
78 aggregate (4 Officer; 73 Enlisted)
Age Range: 16-54

Company A Table 2
Soldiers Not Present March 28, 1863
(Sick, On Leave, AWOL, Detached Duty)

NAME	RANK	AGE	COMMENTS
Obadiah Buckner	Private	23	Fever – hospital Hurricane 02/28/62 to 04/10/63
George H. Fitzwater	Private	18	Died Typhoid at Hurricane Hospital 02/63
Samuel A. Flack	Private	18	Typhoid – Gallipolis Hospital 02/12/1863 to 1864
William B. Greathouse	Private	44	Appointed Hospital Nurse Pt. Pleasant 11/1862
John G. Moore	Private	20	Typhoid - hospital Pt. Pleasant Feb-April 1863
Ralph Pauley	Private	30	Sick at home 11/1862 to 04/1864
George W. Ramsey	Private	29	Sick at home 01/1863 to 04/10/1863; died Pt. Pleasant 07/08/64
Lewis Riffle	Private	35	Typhoid - hospital Pt. Pleasant since 11/1862
Robert H. Snodgrass	Private	17	Enteric Fever – hospital Pt. Pleasant 02/1863-died 09/03/1863
Samuel Snodgrass	Private	49	Father of Pvt Robert Snodgrass; Typhoid, hospital Pt. Pleasant 12/1863 to 06/1863
William Metheny	Private	19	Typhoid – field hospital Hurricane since 02/63
Milton Wilson	Private	36	Detailed hospital nurse Pt. Pleasant since 12/62

Source: CSR, 13th West Virginia Muster Rolls, WV Archives. December 1, 1864 West Virginia Adjutant General Report, Wheeling, WV: J.F. M'Dermot Publishing, pp. 346-348.

APPENDIX C

13TH WEST VIRGINIA VOLUNTEER INFANTRY COMPANY B MUSTER ROLL, APRIL 10, 1863

Company B

NAME	RANK	AGE	COMMENTS
Milton Stewart	Captain	19	Promoted Lt. Col. 11/01/1864
Lovell C. Rayburn	1st Lt.	23	
Joseph Butler	2d Lt.	35	
Charles F. Latham	2d Lt.	20	Fever- hosp. Pt. Pleasant 01/1863 to 02/1863
William Greenlee	1st Sgt.	20	Sick- hosp. Pt. Pleasant 11/1862 to 01/1863
Alfred F. Sullivan	Sergeant	20	
Calvin F. Blessing	Corporal	17	
Robert O. Boggess	Corporal	20	
Robert Eckard	Corporal	21	
William Lawson	Corporal	18	
Samuel C. Love	Corporal	20	
James A. Rayburn	Corporal	25	WIA slightly in head in action 03/28/1863
Spencer Adkins	Private	33	
George H. Adkinson	Private	22	
David Bailey	Private	41	
Fisher Barnette	Private	24	AWOL 02/24 to 03/17 to see sick brother

Samuel Barnette	Private	24	
William Barnette	Private	24	
James Barnette	Private	18	
Preston Barnette	Private	20	
John W. Bailey	Private	21	Killed by citizen May 28, 1863
Enoch Casto	Private	18	
Mason Casto	Private	18	
Oscar Chapman	Private	19	
Mathias Cullins	Private	18	Also spelled Collis
William T. DeWeese	Private	25	
Calvin J. Eckard	Private	19	
William Edwards	Private	44	
James M. Fawser	Private	17	
Andrew W. Ferguson	Private	37	
John H. Ferguson	Private	17	
Daniel M. Fisher	Private	22	
John H. Fisher	Private	24	
John M. Fisher	Private	23	
Thomas H. Fisher	Private	22	
James H. Gaskins	Private	21	
Jesse Hart	Private	18	KIA 03/28/1863 Hurricane Bridge
Eli Jeffers	Private	30	
Felix Jeffers	Private	24	
Gideon Jeffers	Private	22	
James Jeffries	Private	24	
Abraham Johnson	Private	35	
Robert B. Marshall	Private	30	KIA Winchester 09/19/1864
Isaiah McCoy	Private	34	
Alexander McDaniel	Private	18	
John McDaniel	Private	33	
Reuben McDaniel	Private	21	
James McDermitt	Private	20	

APPENDIX C

Henry A. Meek	Private	18	
William H. Mourning	Private	18	
Austin Neville	Private	31	
John T. Oldaker	Private	28	
Preston Newell	Private	29	
Spencer Pickens	Private	30	
William J. Pillow	Private	18	
George W. Plants	Private	18	Fever – sick at home 01/1863 to 02/1863
James A. Rayburn	Private	19	Slightly wounded in head in action Hurricane
Abjah Rhoades	Private	23	
Harrison Rice	Private	18	
Adam W. Roberts	Private	21	Enlisted 03/01/1864 at Hurricane Bridge
Paul Schools	Private	24	
Samuel Smith	Private	26	
William P. Smith	Private	20	
John Smoot	Private	18	
Alfred Sinclair	Private	23	
Henry J. Sines	Private	28	
Anderson Waller	Private	18	
Alexander H. Weinbriener	Private	24	
Robert Young	Private	30	Blacksmith
Adolphus Wood	Private	19	Sick hospital Hurricane 12/1862 to 01/1863
Ultimus Young	Private	18	KIA 03/28/1863 Hurricane Bridge

Company B Statistics
71 aggregate (Officer, Enlisted)
Aggregate Age Range: 17-44

Company B Table 2
Soldiers Not Present March 28, 1863
(Sick, On Leave, AWOL, Detached Duty)

NAME	RANK	AGE	COMMENTS
William Ball	Private	21	Typhoid – hospital Hurricane 02/28/1863 to 04/10/1863
Christopher C. Barnette	Private	16	Pneumonia – died home 02/1863
Patrick Caldwell	Private	23	Typhoid – died hospital Hurricane 04/18/1863
Charles Carroll	Private	34	Detached as Teamster
William R. Eckard	Corporal	21	Pneumonia – home 01/1863 to 04/1864
Harrison Frost	Private	39	Sick – hospital Pt. Pleasant 10/1862 to 10/1863 discharged
William Knapp	Private	35	Fever – sent home 01/1863 to 04/10/1863
Josiah Mattox	Private	29	Sick - sent home 01/1863 to 04/10/1863
Tobias L. Mathis	Private	22	Diarrhea - sent home 01/1863 to 04/10/1863
James McCoy	Private	17	Sick hospital Pt. Pleasant 02/1863 to 05/1863
Lorean Olinger	Private	22	Typhoid – hospital Hurricane 02/1863 to 06/1863
Peter M. Rhoades	Private	22	Fever – sent home 01/1863 to 04/10/1863
Nelson O. Rice	Private	28	Typhoid/Pneumonia died hospital Pt. Pleasant 11/1862
Vincent D. Rice	Private	27	Sick hospital Pt. Pleasant since 10/1862; discharged 02/1863 due to disability
John Riddle	Private	23	Fifer – removed 12/1862; Pneumonia – sent home 01/1863 to 09/1863

Nehemiah Shinn	Private	25	Typhoid – hospital Pt. Pleasant since 02/1863
William Wamsley	Private	23	Sick – hospital Pt. Pleasant 01/1863 to 06/1863
Ezekial H. Wilson	Private	37	Detached as Cook at Pt. Pleasant Hospital 10/1862 to 1865
Daniel Wolfe	Private	25	Typhoid – hospital Hurricane 01/1863 to 04/1863; moved to Pt. Pleasant hospital
John Waugh	Private	44	Captured at Pt. Pleasant by enemy 03/30/1863 and paroled

Source: CSR, 13th West Virginia Muster Rolls, WV Archives. December 1, 1864 West Virginia Adjutant General Report, Wheeling, WV: J.F. M'Dermot Publishing, pp. 348-350.

APPENDIX D

13TH WEST VIRGINIA VOLUNTEER INFANTRY COMPANY D MUSTER ROLL, APRIL 10, 1863

Company D			
NAME	**RANK**	**AGE**	**COMMENTS**
Simon Williams	Captain	28	Fever – 04/10/1863 to 05/1863
George Snowden	1st Lt.	22	
Hezekiah Scott	Sergeant	23	Color Sergeant
John M. Graham	Sergeant	30	
Michael Roseberry	Sergeant	35	
John Barcus	Corporal	29	
Thomas Campbell	Corporal	26	
Richard W. Meeks	Corporal	20	
George F. Miller	Corporal	34	
Francis A. Mills	Corporal	18	
James Robinson	Corporal	19	
William Swain	Corporal	32	Detached hunting deserters 02/28/1863 to 03/12/1863
George S. Arnold	Private	19	
Lewis A. Arnold	Private	18	
Lewis C. Barnes	Private	19	
James Barnette	Private	19	
John Bishop	Private	34	

Nathaniel Burchfield	Private	34	Deserted 06/1863 from Hurricane Bridge
William Burchfield	Private	36	Deserted 01/10/1863; present 04/10/1863
John Carr	Private	37	Deserted 06/23/1863 from Hurricane Bridge
James A. Cartmill	Private	19	
Henry Cherry	Private	24	
William B. Cherry	Private	16	
William H. Cyrus	Private	29	
John Embleton	Private	24	
George W. Forber	Private	25	
Marion Fry	Private	21	
Peter Fry	Private	31	
Benjamin Geary	Private	43	Detailed Hospital Nurse – Hurricane Bridge 04/11/1863
William B. Geary	Private	16	
Andrew J. Gibbs	Private	18	
George H. Gibbs	Private	26	
Junius R. Gibbs	Private	19	
Sheldon Gibbs	Private	28	
William Jackson	Private	43	Detailed Hospital Nurse – Hurricane Bridge 04/11/1863
Lewis C. Johnson	Private	16	
William Kearns	Private	22	
John Killingsworth	Private	36	
Patrick Klein	Private	35	
William H. Landers	Private	20	
James Linihan	Private	28	
George W. Maggi	Private	40	
John McSherry	Private	36	
Jacob Messic	Private	18	
John Moriarty	Private	23	
Leonard Oliver	Private	44	Detailed ambulance driver 01/1863 to 02/1863; present March

APPENDIX D

Thomas Oliver	Private	24	
John Phelps	Private	42	
Thomas Price	Private	23	
John Silas	Private	35	
Henry Schlosser	Private	18	
Harry F. Sherman	Private	22	Deserted Winfield 01/1862; returned 02/1863
George Smallcomb	Private	29	
Marshall Smith	Private	24	Pneumonia – hospital Hurricane 02/1863; present 03/28/1863
Newman Swain	Private	20	
Andrew Taylor	Private	18	
John Taylor	Private	16	
Jacob Tucker	Private	40	Typhoid - fought ill- hospital Hurricane from 03/30/1863 sent to Pt. Pleasant hospital until end of war – only battle he saw
Henry Vincent	Private	18	
Lewis Vincent	Private	25	
Adam Higgins	Private	25	
George W. Wilson	Private	44	Cook at Pt. Pleasant Hospital 10/1862 to 02/1863

Company D Statistics
Aggregate 62 (2 Officer, 60 Enlisted)*
Age Range: 18-44

Company D Table 2
Soldiers Not Present March 28, 1863
(Sick, On Leave, AWOL, Detached Duty)

NAME	RANK	AGE	COMMENTS
John Blackmon	Private	18	Nurse – sick in Pt. Pleasant Hospital since 02/10/1863
Issac Dingy	Private	31	Sick – hospital Pt. Pleasant 02/11/1863 to 04/11/1863
John Pickens	Private	40	Typhoid – hospital Pt. Pleasant 11/1862 to 1865
Moses Roush	Private	25	Typhoid – hospital Pt. Pleasant 01/1863 to 09/1863
John Smith	Private	30	Fever – hospital Hurricane; moved to Pt. Pleasant 04/20/1863
William Wolfe	Private	42	Fever – hospital Point Pleasant 02/12/1863 to 03/16/1863
Jonathan Zerckle	Private	18	Sick quarters – 12/1862 to 01/1862

Source: CSR, 13th West Virginia Muster Rolls, WV Archives. December 1, 1864 West Virginia Adjutant General Report, Wheeling, WV: J.F. M'Dermot Publishing, pp. 353-356.

Appendix E

13th West Virginia Volunteer Infantry Company H Muster Roll April 10, 1863

Company H			
NAME	RANK	AGE	COMMENTS
Thomas W. Hampton	Captain	36	Resignation accepted 03/10/1863 by General Crook
Oliver Griswold	1st Lt.	26	Took command 03/10/1863
William J. Matthews	1st Lt.	25	Former Adjutant
Joseph Kneff	2d Lt.	32	
Harvey Dunkle	1st Sgt.	28	
Robert H. Clark	Corporal	21	
Wesley W. Crofoot	Corporal	18	
John H. Duke	Corporal	24	
David Lowrey	Corporal	31	
John L. Bench	Private	23	
James C. Blair	Private	29	
Joseph Blair	Private	21	
James P. Burris	Private	19	
Benjamin Burton	Private	19	
James Cartmill	Private	19	
Marshall T.F. Cheverount	Private	23	
George W. Childers	Private	17	

George W. Christian	Private	17	
James F. Christian	Private	19	
Martin V. Coughenhour	Private	22	
Francis M. Crofoot	Private	17	Aka Crowfoot
Samuel Dishnan	Private	18	
James M. Drake	Private	27	
Alexander Elkins	Private	17	
Alexander Eves	Private	20	
James M. Fuller	Private	18	
Peter A. Gardner	Private	25	Sick since 02/1863; did not go to hospital until 04/11/1863
Samuel Gordon	Private	34	
George W. Green	Private	24	
George W. Irby	Private	31	
Andrew J. Jolly	Private	42	
Rice King	Private	19	
Preston C. Lawrence	Private	21	
James McKelly	Private	29	
Peter Miller	Private	44	
Isaac B. Newcomb	Private	28	
Leroy Newman	Private	26	Severely WIA Right Thigh Hurricane Bridge 03/28/1864
Levette Purdue	Private	18	
John Rayder	Private	21	
Albert Ray	Private	19	
Jarret F. Riggs	Private	21	
Spencer Rutherford	Private	23	
Gideon Searles	Private	19	
Jacob Shoemaker	Private	18	Fever 03/1863 did not go to hospital until 04/23/1863
John E. Snyder	Private	19	Fever 02/1863 did not go to hospital until 04/10/1863
Marshall Stanton	Private	21	Enlisted 03/01/1863 at Hurricane Bridge

APPENDIX E

Amos Steel	Private	22	
William Stewart	Private	41	Hospitalized Pt. Pleasant 05/06/63 to 09/1864
Michael Stump	Private	30	Fever hospital Hurricane -01/1863 to 02/1863
Charles Taylor	Private	21	
Archibald Tolbert	Private	37	
Demarcus Ward	Private	17	Right leg shot off by cannonball 10/19/1864
Samuel Weaver	Private	34	
James Weingar	Private	33	
Henry Woolwine	Private	18	
Doliver Workman	Private	17	AWOL 12/1862, returned by 03/1863

Company H Statistics
6 aggregate (3 Officer; 52 Enlisted)
Age Range: 17-44

Company H Table 2
Soldiers Not Present March 28, 1863
(Sick, On Leave, AWOL, Detached Duty)

NAME	RANK	AGE	COMMENTS
John S. Cunningham	2d Lt.	34	with Col. Brown 03/28/1863
William Perdue	2d Lt.	29	Pneumonia- sent home 02/26/1863 to 04/10/1863
Jacob Plybon	Sergeant	24	Pneumonia hospital Pt. Pleasant 02/11/1863 to 04/1863
William M. Crook	Corporal	18	Typhoid hospital Hurricane since 02/11/1863
Hiram Fuller	Corporal	21	Fever – hospital Pt. Pleasant since 12/1862
Henry T. Owen	Corporal	27	Typhoid – hospital Pt. Pleasant since 01/1863
Andrew J. Allen	Private	35	Deserted 02/13/1863
Joel Canterbury	Private	25	Typhoid hospital Pt. Pleasant since 02/14/1863
James P. Elkins	Private	19	Fever – hospital Pt. Pleasant 02/11/1863 to 04/11/1863
Stephen Fuller	Private	34	Typhoid – hospital Pt. Pleasant 02/1863
George W. Fulwiller	Private	38	MIA – presumed deserter during battle 03/28/1863
Albert A. Jameson	Private	16	Typhoid – hospital Pt Pleasant 02/11/1863 discharged 06/1863
Benjamin F. Kimberling	Private	16	Deserted 03/06/1863 from Hurricane Bridge
John E. Hall	Private	44	Typhoid – hospital Hurricane since 02/11/1863
Monterville Perdue	Private	18	Died hospital Pt. Pleasant 11/1862
James C. Plybon	Private	27	Fever – hospital Pt. Pleasant 02/11/1863 to 04/10/1863

APPENDIX E

William T. Shaver	Private	18	Sick 12/1862 sent home – never returned -deserter
Oliver Taylor	Private	21	Typhoid – hospital Pt. Pleasant since 01/1863
Harrison Thacker	Private	28	AWOL 02/1863; present 04/10/1863
Issac West	Private	18	Died hospital Pt. Pleasant 01/23/1863

Source: CSR, 13th West Virginia Muster Rolls, WV Archives. December 1, 1864 West Virginia Adjutant General Report, Wheeling, WV: J.F. M'Dermot Publishing, pp. 364-366.

APPENDIX F

8TH VIRGINIA CAVALRY, COMPANY C TROOPS PRESENT MARCH 28, 1863

Company C				
NAME	RANK	AGE	DOE	COMMENTS
Richmond G. Bourne	Capt		04/27/62	CV Article Vol. XXIV, p. 259
Joseph T. Hampton	1 Lt		01/62	From Mercer Co
S.D. Forest	1st Lt			Listed in Payne's Brigade 02/65
Spotswood D. Moore	1st Lt		04/27/62	
W.M. Dickinson	2d Lt		01/62	
Thomas J. Edwards	2d Lt		04/27/62	WIA 08/02/64
John Austin	2d Lt		04/27/62	POW Shepherdstown 07/03/64; Ft. Delaware
Peyton H. Cornett	3d Lt	26	04/27/62	WIA 06/25/63; discharged for GSW 08/01/63
S.E. Boyer	1st Sgt		04/27/62	WIA 08/15/64 furloughed
J.W. Boyer	Sgt		04/27/62	
James W. Eichelberger	Sgt			Trans from 8th Va Infy
David O'Daniel	Sgt	32	04/27/62	
P.C. Funk	Sgt		04/27/62	Reduced to ranks 09/64; Farmer
John Pridemore	Sgt		04/27/62	WIA; Blacksmith; discharged w/disability

Peter O.J. Thomas	Sgt		04/27/62	POW 08/07/64 Moorefield; Pt Lookout to 03/65
Wiilburn Carr	Cpl		04/27/62	
Wm. P. Goings	Cpl		04/27/62	
C.F. Moore	Cpl		04/27/62	
George Anderson	Pvt	24	04/24/62	Oath 03/30/65
Jesse Anderson	Pvt	22	04/24/62	POW
Wm. F. Anderson	Pvt	19	04/27/62	POW Bunker Hill 09/02/64 Died Measles 04/09/65
James Beaver	Pvt	53		POW 10/62 Putnam Co. Camp Chase, exchanged 12/62
Thornton Bourn	Pvt		04/27/62	POW; surrendered Appomattox
Wm. A. Bourn	Pvt		04/27/63	AWOL 06/63
Wm. M. Bourn	Pvt		04/27/63	Wagon driver
Ephraim Boyer	Pvt	31	04/24/62	Absent sick ? POW Camp Chase
Harvey Boyer	Pvt		04/27/62	
M.F. Boyer	Pvt		04/27/62	Teamster – may have been detached 63
J.W. Brewer	Pvt		04/27/62	AWOL 10/64
L.P. Brewer	Pvt	33	04/27/62	Teamster; POW 09/22/64, Ft. Delaware to 02/65
Charles L. Carr	Pvt		04/27/62	From Grayson Co. Va
H.S. Carr	Pvt		07/62	
J.J. Carr	Pvt		04/27/62	
Andrew Carrico	Pvt	26	04/27/62	POW Moorefield 08/64, from Grayson Co. Va.
Wm. A. Carrico	Pvt	24	04/27/62	Captured & released Lewisburg 05/23/62
Stephen C. Combs	Pvt		04/27/62	POW 07/29/64, Oath 06/65
Eli Cornett	Pvt		04/27/62	

APPENDIX F

Name	Rank	Age	Date	Notes
Fielding R. Cornett	Pvt	27	04/27/62	WIA 09/16/64, from Grayson Co. Va. Left Letters UVA
George W. Cornett	Pvt	22	04/27/62	Deserted 09/18/64
L.D. Cornett	Pvt		04/27/62	AWOL 06/63 to 09/63
Noah Cornett	Pvt		04/27/62	
S.M. Cornett	Pvt		04/27/62	Deserted 07/64
Stephen Cornett	Pvt		04/27/62	WIA & Captured 08/19/63; Pt. Lookout to 10/30/64
W.J. Cornett	Pvt		04/27/62	AWOL 06/30/63
D.N. Cox	Pvt		11/01/63	Enl. Taylorsville TN
J.M. Cox	Pvt		05/27/62	Deserted 09/64
Wm. M. Crawford	Pvt		04/27/62	AWOL 14 days; transferred from 26 Bttn Va Inf
Z.S. Daniels	Pvt		04/27/62	
James Dunivant	Pvt		04/27/62	AWOL 10/13 to 10/21/63
M. Eisler	Pvt		04/27/62	POW Strausburg 09/23/64; Pt Lookout 10/13/64
Henry W. Fields	Pvt	18	04/27/62	Enl. Age 16; b. Randolph Co. NC; POW 06/64 to 02/65
Issac Fields	Pvt		04/27/62	
Z. Flannigan	Pvt		04/27/62	POW Moorefield 08/07/64
Samuel Foster	Pvt		04/27/62	WIA 08/07/64; Blacksmith
K.B. Funk	Pvt		04/27/62	Teamster; Deserted 09/01/64
Alex H. Furrow	Pvt			POW Camp Chase; died there 01/65
A.S. Gentry	Pvt		04/27/62	Deserted 10/01/64; also spelled Gintry
E.W. Gruar	Pvt		04/27/62	AWOL 09/21/64 to 10/10/64
John Hale	Pvt		05/05/62	AWOL 09/21/64 to 10/10/64

Name	Rank	Age	Date	Notes
Mintree Hale	Pvt		04/27/62	AWOL 55 days, 64, 07/20 to 09/15; tried & returned to duty
Byram Hall	Pvt		04/27/62	WIA 08/07/64, furloughed from hospital
Creed L. Hanks	Pvt	24	04/27/62	Gov't agent Dublin 07/62; Harness maker 01/64
Henry F. Hanks	Pvt		04/27/62	POW 10/20/64; Appomattox; brother of Creed Hanks
Martin Hanks	Pvt		04/27/62	Brother of Henry and Creed; detach. Mail carrier 07/63
H.E. Higgins	Pvt		04/27/62	
Stephen C. Holmes	Pvt		04/27/62	POW Chambersburg 07/31/64; Ft Delaware
Minitree Isom	Pvt		04/27/62	AWOL 55 days 10/31/64
J.J. Johnson	Pvt		04/27/62	AWOL 8 days 10/27/63
Stephen Johnson	Pvt	19	04/27/62	POW 08/07/64 Moorfield; died 12/64 Camp Chase
Wallace Johnson	Pvt		04/27/62	
E.T. Kirby	Pvt		04/27/62	Deserted 10/01/64
Joel Kirby	Pvt		04/27/62	Deserted 07/01/64
John Kirby	Pvt			Deserted 08/09/64
Crocket Leonard	Pvt	24	04/27/62	POW 08/64; died Camp Chase 02/65 pneumonia
Harrison Leonard	Pvt		04/27/62	AWOL 45 days 08/64
J. McAboy	Pvt			Trans to Chimborazo 10/07/64
Nickolas McKnight	Pvt	33	04/27/62	AWOL 09/28 to 10/15/64
O.J. Moore	Pvt		03/27/62	Died 06/19/64
D.R. Nelson	Pvt		04/27/62	Transferred to 29th Bttn Cav 64
J.W. Nelson	Pvt		04/27/62	AWOL 05/30 to 09/15/64
Martin M. Nelson	Pvt		04/27/62	

APPENDIX F

W. H. Nelson	Pvt		04/27/62	AWOL 5/64 to 9/64 – arrested
Wm. S. Nuckolls	Pvt		04/27/62	WIA 07/29/64; only partially recovered in 1868
J.M. Perkins	Pvt		04/27/62	POW 08/07/64 Moorefield
Elisha Perry	Pvt		04/27/62	AWOL 01/20 to 09/20/64
James H. Porter	Pvt		04/27/62	POW Cabell Co. 04/05/63; died Camp Chase 10/63
Hugh Roberts	Pvt		04/27/62	AWOL 06/62 to 09/62
James Roberts	Pvt		04/27/62	
John Roberts	Pvt		04/27/62	AWOL 08/15/ to 09/15/6??
Logan Roberts	Pvt		04/27/62	
J.D. Robinson	Pvt		04/27/62	AWOL 14 days 1862
Wm. Robinson	Pvt		04/27/62	AWOL 14 days 1862
Mark Sesler	Pvt		04/27/62	Blacksmith; POW 10/09/64 Pt. Lookout to 65
Layfayette Slusher	Pvt		04/27/62	Deserted 07/01/64
Creed South	Pvt		04/27/62	Deserted 07/64
James R. South	Pvt		04/27/62	Deserted 09/01/64
James Taylor	Pvt		04/27/62	Bugler; AWOL 06/64 to 09/64
John Taylor	Pvt		04/27/62	AWOL 14 days 10/31/64
John C. Taylor	Pvt.		04/21/62	Greenbrier Co resident
Joseph Taylor	Pvt		04/27/62	AWOL 06/64
Robert Taylor	Pvt		04/27/62	
Milton G. Trent	Pvt		04/27/62	Detached agriculturist 09/17/64
Columbus Trimble	Pvt		04/27/62	AWOL 85 days from 10/31/64
George W. Warrick	Pvt		04/27/62	Teamster
Stephen Warrick	Pvt		04/27/62	

Wm. Warrick	Pvt		04/27/62	POW 07/19/64 Harper's Ferry; died Elmira 05/22/65
A. Williams	Pvt		04/27/62	Chimborazo 02/20/65
Joseph Yarber	Pvt			

NOTES: Regimental Adjutant was Lt. Wythe Bane Graham, aged 23 on 03/28/63; enl. 07/20/61 at Wytheville Va. WIA 09/24/64, farmer after war. Attended Emory and Henry College. Dr. William Jenkins, AG's brother, enlisted Co E in 1861 and became surgeon 8th Va. Cav. Age 35 in 1863. John T. Johnson, Chaplain, enl. 06/06/62; H.M. Jones QM sergeant 05/25/61 at Wytheville; forage master.

8th Virginia Cavalry, Company C
Sick, AWOL or Detached Duty March 28, 1863

Company C				
NAME	RANK	AGE	DOE	COMMENTS
Joshua Austin	Pvt		04/27/62	Escort Gen. Loring from 02/01/63; Shoemaker
Wm. Austin	Pvt		04/27/62	Escort Gen. Loring from 02/01/63; KIA 10/64
Leonard Crocket	Pvt		04/27/62	Extra duty as Shoemaker Salem, Va. 01/63
Dennis Funk	Pvt			Absent Sick
A.J. Grear	Pvt		04/27/62	Escort Gen. Loring from 02/01/63; deserted 64
Sam'l MacCamant	Pvt		04/27/62	Escort Gen. Loring from 02/01/63
Wm. Padgett	Pvt		04/27/62	Escort Gen. Loring from 02/01/63; Shoemaker
Rufus Pierce	Pvt		04/27/62	Sick from 07/62
Isaiah Rector	Pvt		04/27/62	Sick from 07/62; POW 12/64 to 01/65
William Roberts	Pvt		04/27/62	Escort Gen. Loring from 02/01/63
G.W. Ross	Pvt		04/27/62	Sick from 07/62
R.J. Rouse	Pvt	31	04/27/62	Sick from 07/62; d/c 07/24/63 long standing ill
Wyly W. Shaylar	Pvt		04/27/62	Sick from 07/62
John Smith	Pvt		04/27/62	Shoemaker/Blacksmith at Salem from 01/63
Granvel South	Pvt		04/27/62	Escort Gen. Loring from 02/01/63
Grandvil Stamper	Pvt		07/27/61	Sick from 07/62; d/c 04/07/63 disability
Daniel A. Taylor	Pvt	21	04/27/62	POW Putnam Co. 09/24/62; Camp Chase 10/27

Source: CSR, 8th Virginia Cavalry, RG 94, M324, Rolls 81-86, National Archives.

APPENDIX G

Union Casualties at Hurricane Bridge

13th West Virginia Volunteer Infantry
March 28, 1863

COMPANY	KILLED	WOUNDED
A	2	2
B	2*	6
D	0	1
H	0	1
Total	4	10

[*] Adjutant 1st Lieutenant Emery Bridgeman was mortally wounded. He was a member of Company A and the 13th West Virginia Infantry Adjutant.

Note only four of the wounded are identified in sources available at the time of this publication.

Source: Records of the Adjutant General's Office (Record Group 94), Book Records of Union Organizations, 13th West Virginia Infantry, Vol. 4 of 4, Morning Reports, Companies A-D, F-K, March-February 1863. Accession No. E112-115, PI-17. National Archives, Washington DC.

Name Index

Abbott, Joel 113
Ambler, Irene 123
Bailey, David 39
Barbee, Andrew 64
Barnette, Christopher 44
Barnette, Fisher 67
Bays, Harry 150
Baxter, Michael 68
Benedict, Samuel 116, 168
Bloss, Hiram 158
Blundon, Edgar 119, 153
Bowyer, George C. 12
Bridgeman, Austin 115
Bridgeman, Emory J. 103, 115, 116, 117, 168
Brown, William R. 29, 30, 31, 32, 40, 41, 44, 63, 67, 101, 102, 105, 109, 116, 117, 133, 138, 139, 153, 159, 161, 167, 168, 171
Budd, William 68
Burchfield, Nathan 39, 40, 43, 67
Burnside, Ambrose E. 11
Burrows, David 17, 158, 171
Caldwell, Patrick H. 66, 75
Campbell, Thomas M. 43
Cargill, George W. 63
Cargill, Samuel G. 63
Carr, John 39
Carter, John D. 46, 133, 134, 136, 146, 148, 150, 151, 153

Chapman, John R. 120
Cherry, William B. 44
Cobb, Francis A. 68
Copenshaver, Thomas 108, 162
Conner, Fred 41, 99, 101, 134
Corns, James M. 41, 75, 76, 87, 101
Corns, William 77
Cowen, Benjamin R. 134
Cox, Jacob Dolson 11, 12, 13, 14, 16, 17, 18, 19, 20, 21, 22, 29, 42, 133, 136, 137
Crook, George 11, 20, 21, 22, 29, 32
Crook, William M. 68
Cunningham, John S. 116, 168
Daley, Charles D. 31
Davis, Jefferson 136
Dawson, Charles M. 39
Edens, Martin V.B. 53, 55, 101, 105, 123
Estes, Jack 86
Estes, James M. 86, 87
Farley, Henry 116
Ferguson, Milton J. 4, 41, 75, 80, 158, 159, 162
Fitzwater, George W. 68
Floyd, John B. 20, 80
Ford, Fred 134, 135, 148, 149
Foster, Elmer 123

209

Fulwiller, George W. 109
Gaskins, James H. 43
Gaskins, Samuel 43
Gatewood, Perry 65
Geary, Benjamin 65
Gibson, Calvary 2
Gordon, Samuel 68
Griffith, John xxi, 122
Griffith, Lewis xxi, 122
Griffith, Rachel xxi, 122
Griswold, Oliver W. 4, 40, 41
Gutherie, Edward S. 137
Hall, James R. 4, 18, 19, 30, 42, 78, 79, 170, 171
Hankins, Jonathan 113
Hansford, Victoria Teays 6, 8
Hampton, Taylor H. 40
Hart, Jesse 117
Hawkins, William N. 139
Hayes, Rutherford B. 160
Hess, John H. 52, 54, 103, 158
Hess, Samantha 158
Higginbotham, Cynthia xxii
Hill, Ambrose P. 12
Hoffman, Henry 115
Holderby, George W. 137
Huddleston, Samuel 17
Huntington, Collis P. 122
Hurel, William 38
Imboden, John D. 73, 100
Jackson, Thomas J. "Stonewall" 160
Jenkins, Albert G. xix, 16, 44,54, 55,66,73,74,75,77,81, 82, 87, 88, 89, 102, 103, 105, 107, 108, 113, 121, 122, 123, 134, 135, 138, 146, 147, 153, 159, 161, 162, 163, 164, 169, 170
Johnson, Edward 149
Johnson, James W. xix, 30, 31, 45, 46, 47, 52, 53, 54, 64, 80, 101, 102, 105, 107, 108, 109, 110, 113, 120, 121, 122, 133, 137, 154, 157, 159, 160, 161, 162, 163, 169
Johnson, Lewis C. 44
Jones, William "Grumble" 74, 100
Jones, Samuel 73, 80, 81, 82, 89, 164
Keaton, William 2,3
Kelley, B.F. 40, 170
Kennedy, Robert P. 20, 21
Kirby, Hiram 78
Lee, Robert E. 12, 14, 75
Lightburn, James A.J. 11, 14, 15
Love, David 159
Lincoln, Abraham xix, 12, 16
Loring, William 8, 14, 15, 16, 20
McCausland, John 81, 82
Montague, Dudley S. 21
Morgan, John Hunt 73, 160
Morris, Benjamin 78
Morris, Jordan T. 120, 121
Morris, Thomas H. 120, 121
Newman, Leroy 115
Noel, Roderick R. 88, 89
Nounnan, James 8, 9, 77, 101, 162
Nunley, Abner 44
Payne, John 101, 120
Pierpont, Francis H. 12, 16, 19, 20, 116, 138
Ratliff, Robert K. 136

NAME INDEX

Rayburn, James 117
Reno, Jesse 11
Rice, Nelson O. 67
Ricketts, Lucien C. 87, 88
Roberts, Adam 38
Rucker, George 133
Samuels, Alexander H. 101, 102, 124, 137, 138, 139, 146
Samuels, Henry J. 12
Sands, Henry 119
Sands, Matthew 119
Scammon, Eliakim P. 11, 29, 31, 46, 79, 133, 146, 148, 164
Schenck, Robert S. 137, 138, 146
Scott, Hezekiah 103, 105
Sedinger, James D. 88, 89, 101, 120, 136, 137, 139, 161
Shaw, Judith 63
Shaw, Mary 63
Shaw, Mattie 63
Shaw, Rebecca 63, 64
Shaw, Samuel G. 63, 64, 65, 66, 108, 115, 117, 120, 154, 157, 158, 159
Shoemaker, Jacob 32
Smith, Charles W. 136
Smith, David 44
Spurlock, Hurston 3, 4, 158, 159
Stephenson, Nancy xxi
Stephenson, Sarah A. xxii
Stewart, Charles A. 87
Stewart, Harrison D. 87
Stewart, Henry W. 87
Stewart, Milton 31, 32, 46, 102, 117
Stewart, Thomas H. 87
Stewart, William Jr. 87
Stote, Frank 150
Sunderland, John Patrick 82
Sweeney, James 159
Tackett, Lewis xxi
Taylor, John 44
Thompson, Amazetta 17
Thompson, Julia A. M. 18
Thompson, Robert N.B. 18
Timmons, Charles 77, 99, 138
Waggener, Andrew 138
Washington, George xx
Whitworth, Joseph 107
Williams, John S. 138
Winkey, John 78
Wintz, Philip Jr. 38
Witcher, John S. 2, 3
Workman, Dolison 39
Wright, Stape 150
Young, Alexander xxii
Young, Altimus 119
Young, Emilie 8, 9
Young, Jacob R. xxi, xxii
Young, John V. xxii, 8, 9, 20, 21, 22, 42, 77, 116, 153, 167, 168, 169, 170, 171
Young, Nancy xxii
Young, Samuel E. xxii
Young, Sarah F. 8, 9, 10, 119, 153

About the Author

Philip Hatfield, Ph.D., is a member of the Company of Military Historians, and holds a doctorate in psychology from Fielding University; a master's degree in psychology from Marshall University; and a bachelor's degree in psychology and history from the University of Charleston. Dr. Hatfield is a veteran of the U.S. Air Force and is the author of five books and numerous scholarly articles related to the Civil War. He is a native of Hurricane, West Virginia.

35th Star Publishing
www.35thstar.com

www.ingramcontent.com/pod-product-compliance
Lightning Source LLC
Chambersburg PA
CBHW061254110426
42742CB00012BA/1909